# Whoa you donkey...WHOA!

## Adventures of a Lady Prospector

Laura Leveque Alias Jackass Jill

# Whoa you donkey...WHOA!
## Adventures of a Lady Prospector

### Laura Leveque

Copyright 2006 by
Laura Leveque (Levesque).
All rights reserved. This book, or parts thereof,
may not be reproduced in any form
without permission.

ISBN 0-9776444-0-5

Cover design
JacDonald Jones
Bette Waters

Cover Photo
Soska

Book Design
Bette Waters

Drawings by
Leah Patton, Editor
*The Brayer*, Journal of the
American Donkey and Mule Society

Jackass Junction Publishing
4815 Silver City Highway NW
Deming, NM 88030

## Table of Contents

| | |
|---|---|
| Donkey Prospectors Strike Paydirt | 9 |
| Fat Worms | 11 |
| Whoa! You Donkeys, Whoa! | 13 |
| Just Another Gold Trail Day | 14 |
| A Miner's Menu | 17 |
| Firewater Mountain | 19 |
| Rollin, Rollin, Rollin | 21 |
| Land of the '59ers | 23 |
| Moose, Mosquitos, and Gold | 26 |
| A Prospector's Friend | 27 |
| New Mexico or Bust! | 30 |
| Cigars and Black Gold | 33 |
| Mountain Lions and Bighorn Sheep | 36 |
| Locoweed | 40 |
| Tommyknockers | 42 |
| Ladrone | 46 |
| Curly Bill and Skeleton Canyon | 48 |
| Hot High Noon | 52 |
| Searching to Find El Dorado | 55 |
| Don Quoxite and Sancho Panza | 59 |
| Quest | 62 |
| Kelly Mine or Bust | 64 |
| Mule and Donkey Ride and Drive | 67 |
| HIgh Winds Didn't Stop These Asses | 67 |
| Smilin' Jack and the Lost Gold Mine | 69 |
| Camp Cuisine | 71 |
| Desert Winter | 74 |
| The Other Hole-in-the-Wall Gang | 77 |
| Pueblo Springs, New Mexico | 79 |
| San Mateo Mountains | 82 |
| Burro, Donkey, Mule or Ass? | 85 |
| Drywashing | 88 |
| Silver! | 90 |
| Rodeo Tavern | 94 |
| Uncle Wayne and the Labyrinth Mine | 98 |
| Logging in the Zuni Mountains | 102 |
| Soapy and the Black Bear | 106 |
| Alaska Bears | 110 |
| Stacy and the Javelina | 113 |

| | |
|---|---|
| Micro-Gold | 115 |
| Assassin Bug | 117 |
| Dead Meat | 122 |
| Pollyanna's Mountain Lion | 127 |
| California Dreamin' | 129 |
| Boiled Mule | 132 |
| Epilogue | 137 |
| Appendix A<br>  Ore Deposits of the San Juan Mountains | 140 |
| Appendix B<br>  The Hard Tack Mine History | 142 |
| Appendix C<br>  The Ghosts of Rosedale and its Mines | 143 |
| Appendix D<br>  Eliminate Cinch Sores From Your Donkeys | 144 |
| Appendix E<br>  A Few Mining Terms | 146 |
| Appendix F<br>  American Donkey & Mule Society Terminology | 149 |
| About The Author | 153 |

Dedicated to my parents,
Roland Lionel "Frenchie" Levesque (deceased)
and Nora Levesque DiVincenzo, who camped with me and the
donkeys in Colorado the summer after dad died.

## BOOKS BY LAURA LEVEQUE

Prospectors Guide to Mineral Knowledge
and Wealth 1995
Co-Author Lars H. Helm

Prospectors Guide 1996

Adventures of a Donkey Prospector 2003

Whoa you Donkey...Whoa! 2006

Columnist since 1996 for
*Gold Prospectors Magazine*

Contributor
*Brayer Magazine*

Screenplay
Dead Men Drift 2006

# PREFACE

Like many writers I've kept journals (actually spiral notebooks) as long as I can remember. Some were ideas for paintings, notes about travel, and books I've read. The majority of essays and thoughts were of camping expeditions with dogs and later donkeys. After five years in the moving and hauling business, then as fill-in help for federal contracts on a railroad construction crew, and twenty some years as a mural and sign painter—ten to twelve hours a day on a scaffold or ladder—my back had had enough.

I looked at writing as a skill to learn when I could no longer work on large murals and signs. So I studied, studied and studied, and practiced, practiced, practiced. I noticed that building a story was a lot like painting. A non-fiction piece was more like painting a sign, whereas a fiction story was more like a fine art painting.

In 1990 I submitted my first non-fiction article. "Granny Get Your Gun" appeared in *Women & Guns* magazine. The picture of my mom stepping out of her motor home aiming her .357, graced the front cover. I sold a few more short pieces to *Women & Guns*. In 1991 another article "Rudimentary Woodswoman Skills," basic advice for women in the outdoors, was published by *American Survival Guide*. I even got some fan mail on this story.

I relied on good and interesting photos to sell these articles. My mentors were full time writers, Tom Owens and Diana Star Helmer, who lived in Gig Harbor, Washington. Their encouragement and suggestions were priceless. I can walk into any major bookstore and their books adorn the sports, children, and young adult shelves.

In 1992 two sisters in Lakebay, Washington, started a small monthly newspaper, the *Peninsula Post*. Their office was in the same "KC Korral" office complex as my chiropractor's. I offered my services and got a low paying position as a columnist. I wrote "Linda Lancaster's Advice for Singles" though I was married at the time, and "Sows, Cows, and Lots of Bull," funny stories about country living and livestock.

I sent clips of the "Lots of Bull" column with a story to *Gold Prospectors* magazine in 1995. They bought my "Adventure in Idaho" story, and requested I write a humorous column about prospecting.

All the old time prospectors had nicknames and I wanted one. The editor and staff at *Gold Prospectors* tossed around fun names for me. The names Sandy Black (a reference to gold bearing black sand), Opal Clay, and Jackass Jill were finalists. We all agreed that Jackass Jill would fit the column style perfectly. While writing the "Donkey Prospector" column for *Gold Prospectors*, I rewrote the stories and sold them as travel stories to RV magazines and other treasure hunting and gold prospecting magazines as well as reprints to newspapers. Most of the "Donkey Prospector" columns are reprinted in *Brayer* magazine.

After moving to Rodeo, New Mexico in 1996, I met the owners of Blueagle Publishing, a husband and wife team, who created the *StateLine Bulletin*. They reprinted some of my local history pieces and suggested I compile my columns into book form. We comb-bound and sold out the first printing of *Adventures Of A Donkey Prospector*. In 2004 the second printing sold out.

In 2005 while attending a screen writing course at the local college in Deming, New Mexico, I met Bette Waters of Bluwaters Press, who designed and edited this edition, *Whoa You Donkey...Whoa!* Bette is guiding me through the process and fun of publishing and marketing.

Note: In these stories I have loosely used the term "tunnel," an excavation that starts on one side of a mountain and exits somewhere else, instead of the term "drift," an excavation that ends underground.

Laura Leveque
Deming, NM
2005

## DONKEY PROSPECTORS STRIKE PAYDIRT

### 1993, Olympic National Forest, Western Washington

Klondike Mike and I wanted to be real "jackass prospectors;" our rendition of *Burro Bill And Me*, a true story written by Edna Calkins Price. For ten years (1931 to 1941) Edna, Bill and five burros, roamed the deserts of Arizona and California on foot, making friends with prospectors and desert rats. So we bought two cantankerous, spoiled, six year old jennet donkeys. Sarah and Lacey were identical cousins, both brown with white points. Neither even halter broke. I remarked, "No wonder they were so cheap."

We tied the donkeys to a tree, brushed them and put on their thick blankets and brand new sawbuck packsaddles. While cinching up, Sarah pushed me against the tree and the packsaddle slid off the other side. Lacey, Mike's donkey managed to get her blanket and sawbuck over her head and had one huge ear sticking out. I fell to the ground, laughing. Klondike Mike was not amused.

We toiled until dusk, sweating–dirt streaked–exhausted. Saddling and packing two donkeys took us about seven hours.

Sarah and Lacey were born and raised together, inseparable. They peed at the same time, pooped at the same time, went into heat at the same time. They could read each others' minds, and pulled donkey stunts in unison. Sarah would give Lacey a knowing look, and I swear I heard Sarah say, "These humans are well meaning but they're idiots." And as if on cue one, two, three, puff up so the saddles slid off later. Their eyes gleamed, "Ha, ha, ha."

Every evening we led the girls over a sheet of plywood and plastic tarp, under a ladder, tip-toed through a flooded lawn; a makeshift obstacle training course.

The next weekend we started our maiden expedition, the saddling process this time a mere three hours.

Simpson Timber Company owned the land around my cabin. Adjoining Simpson land to the north was the Olympic National Forest. Convenient.

We led the donkeys out the gate and started across the black top road. Lacey tip-toed briskly over the road to the tall grass on the other side. But Sarah jerked hard on the lead rope and I fell sprawled on the highway. First unforseen obstacle, paved road. I pushed, Mike pulled. Mike pushed, I pulled. Logging trucks roared by, jake brakes popped like muffled gun fire.

In *Burro Bill and Me*, and *Horses, Hitches, and Rocky Trails*, the authors mention blindfolds as a training and problem solving technique. We put a jacket over Sarah's eyes and pushed and pulled again. Lacey waited impatiently tied to a tree on the other side. It took two hours to cross the road, our front door fifty feet away.

We started up an overgrown elk trail and a scotch broom branch smacked my donkey in the rear, she bolted and ripped the lead rope out of my ungloved hands. Klondike Mike's donkey jumped around in circles, her pack listed forty-five degrees from top dead center. My donkey finally stopped, her packsaddle and canvas panniers hung under her belly and the breeching and breast collar tight as a straight jacket. Unload and reload? Two more hours! And home only three-hundred feet away, and getting dark. Sighing I said, "Let's make camp and try again tomorrow."

The next day we walked two miles on a good logging road to a wooden bridge. The creek ran deep, swift, and log strewn, no way around this one. We led the donkeys nonchalantly forward, hoping they wouldn't notice the hollow wood sound—we slid to a gravelly stop. Another three and a half hours training session for both man and beast—blindfolds, pulley, two-hundred feet of rope, aching arms, and raw burned hands.

Two days later we plodded home, a message left in our mailbox read, "Saw your donkeys, we are moving and have two donkeys for sale, cheap." The seller swore these donkeys were well trained, so we bought them. Trained? They'd never worked a day in their lives, and needed their hooves trimmed.

Meanwhile the manure pile got larger and the yard smaller, so I put up a sign, "DONKEY DUNG FOR SALE." Olympic Worm Casting Farm bought all they could haul for fifty bucks. The small remaining, but ever growing manure pile had lots of red worms. I gathered up the wrigglers and put them in styrofoam cups and painted another sign, "FAT WORMS HERE."

Paydirt that year wasn't at the bottom of a gold pan.

## FAT WORMS

### Reprinted from The Peninsula Post column, "Sows, Cows, and Lots of Bull"

Pick-up trucks towing small fishing boats swooshed past my cabin. Some of these trucks stopped in my driveway.

I strategically placed sandwich board signs with big blue arrows and bright red letters. FAT WORMS HERE. The letter "o" in worms is a picture of an earthworm shaped like an "o."

I'd seen other signs announcing "We Have Worms." Were these quarantine warnings for airborne ringworm? Or a public notice of internal parasite infestation? The earthworms painted on my signs cleared up the question "What kind of worms?"

I sell lots of fishing worms to folks with lots of fishing poles stuck in truck cab gun racks. Old men and old women wearing old hokey hats covered with rusty fish hooks, colorful fishing flies, and fish pins and buttons which read, "I'd rather be fishing!" They love my fat worms. I love my fat worms too.

Earthworms smell like fresh clean earth. The large masses of squirming worms feel cool and moist to warm human hands. Counting and sorting worms around here is a high honor.

Worms are useful, harmless and endearing. The name for worm raising in fancy books is "vermiculture." Instead of calling ourselves Worm Farmers we're Vermiculturists. (I still can't pronounce it right.)

Birds dine on juicy worms, fish gobble them up, pigs go to depths to root them out . . . hmm I wondered what they taste like. My French Canadian relatives serve escargot (snails) alongside clams and oysters. Could worms provide a fine dining experience? To announce, "Honey, we're having earthworm stir-fry tonight," would not work. I never say "I had snails for lunch," but instead "I ate escargot." I say, "The calamary was seasoned perfectly," instead of "Hey, great squid!" Oh! Worm of the soil. "Ver de Terre." Humble beast! Yum yum!

Ver de Terre, like escargot, must first be washed and soaked in cold water then boiled lightly to remove bits of soil. Ver de Terre are entirely edible, with no bones or gristle to throw away! The subtle chestnut flavor of Ver de Terre lends itself well to all sorts of ingredients and methods of preparation. I've tried "Caesar Salada au Ver de Terre," (using dried and crumbled Ver de Terre instead of bacon bits.) We can't forget, "Canapes Ver de Terre," and "Consomme Ver de Terre."

When you serve a Ver de Terre dish you will impress your family and friends (as I have) with your sense of adventure and worldliness. "Ver de Terre au Fromage Suisse" (baked Ver de Terre mixed with a sauce of melted Swiss cheese), a favorite at cocktail parties. Lightly salted butter fried Ver de Terre takes the place of shoestring potatoes

and Chow Mein noodles, and are a crunchy hit at outdoor barbecues. The Applesauce Surprise Cake, perfect for church bake sales.

## WHOA! YOU DONKEYS, WHOA!
### Nez Perce National Forest, Idaho

It looked so simple, the grizzled prospector in the old photo walked peacefully, his donkey followed serenely. I imagined the man pausing often to glory in the landscape and search the terrain features for prospecting sites. He bent often examining rocks, while his faithful donkey stood calmly nearby, patient. Then they'd stroll on . . .

I wanted a peaceful walk with our donkeys, pausing often to glory in the landscape and search the terrain features for prospecting sites and bend often examining rocks while our faithful donkeys stood nearby, patient . . .

*WHOA! WHOA! SLOW DOWN YOU JACKASSES, WE'RE NOT IN A RACE!* My arms ached trying to hold back five-hundred and sixty muscle bound pounds of vitamin and mineral enriched donkey.

That morning we weighed and balanced the donkeys' panniers, their saddle blankets thick and clean. This can't be right, the "books" say no more than one hundred pounds on the dainty, timid, little equines. And NEVER, NEVER beat a donkey to make him move? WHAT? I am dripping wet with sweat. The donkeys breathed normally, not even damp from exertion.

According to our GPS unit, we just walked (no we were dragged, a forced march) five miles starting at 5,500 feet elevation ending 7,000 feet above sea level.

My hands were swollen; my limbs trembled, I barely had the strength to stand and unpack the donkeys, who upon release rolled and frolicked. I couldn't lift a shovel for two days and hid in my sleeping bag moaning. Klondike Mike ached all over. The elevation and forced uphill march did us in. Who wrote those books about donkeys anyway?

Five days later I said, "Let's carry a couple hundred pounds of rock samples back to base camp that ought to slow them down."

The divided loads consisted of: tent, tarp, lawn chairs, cots, camp stove, alcohol fuel, sleeping bags, canteens, buckets, shovels, sluice box, gold pans, metal detector, rifle, cast iron frying pan, coffee pot, more pots and pans, panning tub, Bisquick, sugar, potatoes, canned food, coffee, hammers, chisels, crow bar, axe, and now lots of rocks, minerals and black sand.

Using a hanging scale I loaded one-hundred-seventy-five pounds on big boned Shaggy. One-hundred-sixty pounds on Willy and tailed him to Shaggy. Mike loaded the trotting twins, Sarah and Lacey, with one-hundred-fifty pounds each. No need to tie them together. They were inseparable.

We started down the switchback mountain trail. *WHOA! WHOA! SLOW DOWN YOU JACKASSES, THIS IS NOT A MARATHON!* Our delicate beasts of burden pushed us downhill and stepped on our heels. We panted and cursed through cracked lips. Blue jeans now worn bare at the knees, boot toes gouged by sharp rocks.

Klondike Mike said, "Hell with this!" So we grabbed two canteens, the rifle, and metal detector; untailed, gathered lead ropes and released the restless fully packed string of donkeys. They trotted down the trail, their loads bouncing and flapping, the sound drifted away into the forest.

We strolled into base camp, the donkeys grazed nearby, all packs somewhat intact except for Shaggy's, he was trying to roll. Willy brayed a greeting and trotted toward us. A peaceful scene from a donkey prospector's camp.


## JUST ANOTHER GOLD TRAIL DAY
### Nez Perce National Forest, Idaho

Tinkling sheep bells woke me. Our donkeys sometimes wore cow bells, so I knew we had visitors. I crawled out of my warm sleeping bag, got dressed, threw wood on the hot coals, and shoved the blackened cold half-full coffee pot into the fire.

Company? Maybe a sheepherder moving his sheep on this cool mountain morning. Instead I saw a man dressed in linen white followed by five large pack goats and a woman also dressed in white linen. A picturesque procession. I dashed for my camera, waved, and shouted, "Good morning!"

The five goats carried small aluminum sawbuck packsaddles, with plastic file box panniers, lightweight tent and sleeping bags, a well used gold pan, and fold-up shovel. The large neutered male goats called wethers, stood clustered close to their shepherds. No halters, no lead ropes; like baby chicks following a broody hen. I heard two goats bleat softly. Willy and the other donkeys trotted to the closest edge of their solar charged polywire corral. Brazen, snorting, stomping, and calling out in raucous screechy honking brays at the dainty diminutive pack animals.

The man spoke first. "Do you have a Forest or topo map we could look at?"

His wife said, "One of the goats ate our map last night."

My mining partner Klondike Mike crawled out of his warm sleeping bag and invited everybody, goats and all, around the campfire. We drank reheated coffee and looked at maps, while the goats ate newspaper. We agreed to meet two days later and swap trail stories. As they left I took more pictures. They were truly picturesque. Stan and Maxine in their early seventies, retired potato farmers, hiked historical trails with their pack goats.

Two days later the pack-trains of goats and donkeys met on the north side of Meadow Creek at the base of Gold Hill. We panned for gold, cracked rocks, pried and snooped in crevices. The donkeys hauled five gallon buckets of gravel to the sluice box.

That evening we sat around the campfire drinking sweet pink sun warmed wine from dented tin cups. The wine came from a plastic bladder dispenser in the cardboard box marked *EMERGENCY FLUIDS*.

We ate steaming not quite done beans and burnt baking soda biscuits in the small rusty gold pans we used as plates. I remarked,

"Now this is good living!" and proposed another toast, while Willy nearby brayed and whined horribly. He stood knee deep in meadow grass, a five gallon bucket full of water in the corral—"Oops! I forgot. If we drink, Willy drinks." I yelled, "Just a minute Willy, I'll get your cup!" A special cup marked, *WILLY'S CUP*. After Willy slurped his wine, I told Stan and Maxine how I discovered Willy's party animal side.

I sipped my wine and said, "The donkeys were entertaining the cousins and nephews at my parents' farm on Fox Island, with rides, stealing hats, and Shaggy's specialty—taking bandannas out of hip pockets. One of Willy's tricks was untying his lead rope then walking around carrying the lead in his mouth, which always got a lot of laughs." I paused and took another sip of wine. "Uncle Jack stood holding a champagne cocktail in his right hand. Willy reached around his shoulder from the back, rolled his tongue like a fat straw and sucked my uncle's drink to the last drop. Uncle and onlookers thought this quite hilarious and he gave Willy three more champagne cocktails. Willy stretched out his neck, lifted his head to the sky and bellowed out a deafening bray.

"I told Uncle Jack that was probably enough booze for Willy, as he was becoming a pest, and might fall onto the picnic table or wander off the end of the dock, and if we kept laughing he'd do it again. He's sort of a Red Skelton in a donkey suit."

The goats didn't seem interested in wine. They preferred paper and pine needles. The other donkeys content with dandelions or an extra scoop of grain.

The campfire crackled and glowed. The sun went down fire red, and the cool night air rolled in.

I babbled on about how picturesque and stunning Stan, Maxine, and the pack goats looked. Then Stan insisted that Klondike Mike, I, and the donkeys were more picturesque. This debate went on along with the wine drinking.

Maxine finally said, "We should all quit arguing because we are all equally picturesque." Everyone agreed with this and suggested another toast.

We eventually stumbled to our tents, to dream of mountain trails and gold nuggets. The end of another gold trail day.

## A MINER'S MENU
## Okanogan Highlands, Eastern Washington

The message scrawled on the greasy coffee stained paper place mat, "Get your asses up here, need help hauling some rock. Uncle Wayne."

Our donkey pack train took the old fire trail short cut toward Uncle Wayne's eighty acre homestead and mine on Maryann Creek in the Okanogan Highlands. We stopped at Wayne's 1952 rusted Chevy truck, ugly but solid, parked about two miles from his "ranch." Most the summer a four-wheel drive, tractor, or his mules hauled fuel in. We filled two 5-gallon jerry cans from the fifty-five gallon fuel drums in the truck bed at the end of the passable road.

The donkeys clip-clopped on the dusty boulder strewn and washed out road, a light breeze whooshed through the pines like bird wings, the tamaracks glowed bronze, the quaking aspen rustled and shimmered yellow . . . then we heard the generator. I hated that noisy thing, hauling fuel in was a pain, but we couldn't run the rock crusher, welder, and other stuff without it.

Wayne kept twenty or so head of Scottish Highland, Hereford, and Longhorn cross beef cattle, a flock of laying hens, four hogs, and 2 thirty-some year old draft mules. Maude, the molly mule was about blind, but worked fine with Harold, the john mule. Harold split a hoof and couldn't work for awhile. So Wayne sent for us and our donkeys to move boulders and haul rocks to the crusher before winter set in.

The best gold of course was in the steepest most rattlesnake infested ravine on the entire property. The days were shorter and cooler, wouldn't be much snake trouble.

Willy once stomped a rattler and flung it twenty-five feet. Uncle Wayne was a little bit ticked because Willy's sharp hooves wrecked some of the meat and skin.

A World War II vintage D-8 cable blade dozer tilted near forty-five degrees on a ledge, suspended, a twisted track dangled. Uncle Wayne dubbed her *Lady Albatross*. Wayne said, "Alba's been hanging there about twelve years." We all took bets on which month it would finally flop over. "I just got tired of welding and sledgehammering on the darn thing!" Wayne like most backcountry mechanics depended on sledgehammers for repairs and fine alignment of parts.

Klondike Mike asked Wayne, "What's for dinner besides snake stew?"

Uncle Wayne laughed, "You're a few hours late, a gal hiked through here this morning. A vegetarian save the endangered rat type, combat boots and layers of long skirts, left some togu or something like that."

"Oh, you mean tofu," Mike said.

"Yea, that's it. Soybean cheese I guess? I told her I'd rather have a big rare steak and about six fresh fertilized eggs and she said I was a merciless carnivore!" Uncle Wayne laughed. "I told her real Americans feed this soybean stuff to hogs! She got a little huffy, but stayed long enough to boil up some herbal tea...Looked like something I dug out of the mule's hoof. Well I was gunna try it just to be polite, but it smelled like moldy hay and chicken droppings. If that's health food, I told her, I'll stay unhealthy.

"I'll get a ham out of the smokehouse and fry up some potatoes and onions in bacon grease. Mike, you can take care of the donkeys and look at Harold's split hoof while me and Jill rustle up dinner and plan the Thanksgiving menu."

Uncle Wayne dug out his well worn *Concise Encyclopedia of Gastronomy* by Andre Simon. I thumbed through it and read aloud: "Eel Pie, Frogs, hmm, I didn't know frogs were considered a fish dish? Turtle Soup. 'Bear paws are a celebrated delicacy and are, I believe, cooked best in the ashes of a wood fire by the man who shot the bear.' Bat? 'There are those who have tried the bat and found it taste like a house mouse, only mousier.'" I was laughing hard and had to sit down. "Monkey, Muskrat (when used for food is called Marsh Rabbit), Opossum, Pig's Ears, Pig's Trotters, and Rat.

"'Rats are not a dainty dish to set before a King; but for a really hungry man, they're just the very thing!' Uncle Wayne, where did you get this book? It's hysterical!" I continued, "Blackbird Pie, Badger, and Equus Asinus, the Ass. Quote: 'Donkey meat was like mutton in colour, firm and savoury. I can most solemnly assert that I never wish to taste a better dinner than joint of donkey, or a ragout of cat . . . '

"Well, Uncle Wayne," I said, "I don't think we should try donkey meat this year because we need them for working , besides that Mike would divorce us, so let's do something totally different and eat a store bought turkey!"

Uncle Wayne thought this was really outrageous and nearly choked.

## FIREWATER MOUNTAIN
### Okanogan National Forest

It was a grand mountain morning. The thin cool air snappy and brilliant.

Lacey's and Sarah's panniers and top packs were loaded and hitched. I tightened the cinch on Willy's McClellan cavalry saddle, and tied Lacey's baling twine lead to a D-ring on the britchen and mounted. Mike rode Shaggy, the big boned spotted gelding. Our cortege plodded through the canyon and climbed switchbacks to Lightning Ridge.

Lacey's packs listed starboard. Her bright colored horse-size polyfoam saddle pad stuck over her rump and neck, she looked like Olive Oil wearing Mae West clothes. I stopped and added rocks to the port side pack as ballast. Then a half hour later the pack hung low on the left, ballast needed on the right.

Mike remarked as he and his donkeys strutted by, "You didn't weigh your panniers this morning did you?" Usually this was my comment to him. It was my turn to eat trailside crow.

I remounted and we followed Mike, Shaggy, and Sarah. Mike's long skinny legs dangled, his boots not a foot from the ground, and myself built like a Hobbit could barely reach the stirrups. This image was too hysterical and I fell off Willy, clutched my belly and tried not to pee my pants. The donkeys were accustomed to this and used the opportunity to graze. I composed myself, mounted, and we trotted after Mike.

Our destination was a mine dump and tunnel on what the locals called Firewater Mountain in the Okanogan National Forest. An old rancher and muleskinner named Sonny had run a still in one of the mine drifts with a spring and good drainage. He turned corn, barley, and potatoes into a clear liquid that ended up in mason jars. I'd see large men in coveralls and knee-high manure covered rubber boots behind the stock pens, each with a quart jar saying things like "Sonny's likker got good bead." They'd shake their jars and stare for a long time at the chain of bubbles strung inside the glass, like a "string of pearls."

Uncle Wayne rallied to Sonny's defense and would pound his fist on the table and recite, "Fermented, brewed, and distilled alcohol is a precious asset, a given right, a downright necessity to soften the harsh edges of reality."

We scrambled up a talus slope to a solid looking mine tunnel above a substantial waste rock dump. Dark, heavy, irony looking minerals. Galena, pyrite, and a green tarnished dense mineral that might be "green gold," a gold, copper, and silver ore. If we roast, crush, and pan the ore we might get some color.

We unloaded the packs and got our battered hard hats with the duct taped head lamps, battery packs held together with rubber bands, the walking sticks for poking in creepy places, rock hammer, extra canteen, flashlights, spare batteries, and a few candles—all necessary items for exploring tunnels.

This tunnel had what miners called a piss ditch. One side of the tunnel floor is lower and the tunnel entrance is always below the rest of the mine workings. Water flows out this shallow ditch and full ore cars roll better to the landing on this slight slope.

The donkeys waited outside while we entered the cool darkness. They stood peering inside but didn't care for narrow wet tunnels. Besides that a donkey with panniers would not fit anyway. A small cart might work. The mine donkeys and mules used during frontier days were raised and trained in tunnels or learned by following older experienced animals. This time we'd drag the sacks and backpacks of ore and supplies out ourselves.

About seven hundred feet into the mountain, the tunnel got larger and arced to the right. Two hundred feet farther was a raise or open stope area. We felt a draft on our necks, meant an air shaft nearby. Fifty more feet we found a large stack of firewood, gunny sacks full of coal, and a bundle of empty sacks on an old wood dolly with metal wheels. Beyond this the glow of a huge, five foot high copper pot resting over an iron firebox; copper tubing, a spring fed gravity water system, two 55 gallon wood barrels, oil lamps, an old wood and canvas cot, and other interesting tools. A shrine to a moonshiner and craftsman.

We left everything alone except the ore we came to collect, and stayed till our lights dimmed.

The donkeys brayed a greeting when we emerged from the tunnel squinting and dragging sacks of rocks.

Last time we heard from Uncle Wayne he wrote, "Sonny's grandson moved back from Alaska, inherited Sonny's ranch and some mining claims. I saw him at the feed store. He had a few sacks of cracked corn, sugar and some other stuff. Thank God! I was gettin tired of that store bought stuff. See you next year. Uncle Wayne."

## ROLLIN, ROLLIN, ROLLIN . . .
### Death Valley, Nevada

"Rollin, Rollin, Rollin, Keep those donkeys rollin, gold pans ." We sang our version of the "Rawhide" song while heading south for the winter. The 5th wheel travel/livestock trailer sagged and swayed. This year more, bigger, and better mining equipment and another donkey. (A stud jack named Bosephus, Bo for short.) But more stuff requires more truck, and our Ford truck was tired and old.

"Rollin, Rollin, Rollin, to the Gila Mountains . . . "

For a pleasant break we camped on BLM land bordering Death Valley. We leaned back in our aluminum lawn chairs and smoked hand rolled Cuban seed Corona Gorda cigars.

Someone asked "Why do you smoke cigars?"

My reply, "Cigar smoke is a natural insect repellent and an herbal relaxation aid." But no insects were biting tonight.

"Mike?"

"Yeah."

"Uncle Wayne said something about the North country; wolves and dog packs being no problem for donkeys. He saw donkeys attack and kill strange dogs. I guess that's why they're used to guard sheep and calves. But he said a lone donkey is no match for a mountain lion, and in Nevada donkey meat is a mountain lion favorite. Our donkeys should be fine. I hope."

We both sat smoking and peering into the twilight waiting for the cat scream, the pounding hooves, the leap, razor teeth, claws, blood, angry donkeys turning to fight... Later the donkeys stopped nibbling brush and watched. All radar ears followed a traveling shape about five hundred feet away. It moved in a slow circle around camp. The shadow circled closer and closer.

"JILL, QUICK, FLIP ON THE OUTSIDE TRAILER LIGHTS. I'LL GRAB THE RIFLE!"

Willy stomped and Bo snorted.

"Mike, it's a feral jack. He's here to check out the jennets."

"Or steal them," Mike replied.

We glanced at our jennets. Both were very round and due to foal in a few months. The girls were not in heat. Our twenty one year old pampered jack no match for this tough feral jack.

Willy pawed the ground and Bo snorted like a bull moose. The feral jack, ears flat back, bared his teeth, lowered his head and charged Bo. The hormone filled jack paid no attention to our yelling and banging aluminum chairs against the trailer.

Should we fire in the air? Should we shoot him?

But before any shots were fired Mike yelled, "OPEN THE TRAILER DOOR NOW!"

The wild jack had Bo by the neck and they were running toward us. Willy attacked the jack from the side. The girls brayed. I swung the rear door open, then rolled under the trailer. Bo skidded and hit the side of the trailer. The feral jack lost his grip while trying to shake Willy's bites and kicks. Bo recovered and leapt into the trailer. Mike dove for the door and slammed it shut. The jennets not impressed kicked and drove the jack into the desert night.

We put the polywire corral fence back up, and hung bells on it and left Bo inside for the night.

"Well," Mike said, "That's the fastest I've ever seen Bo load up!"

We retrieved our scattered lawn chairs and searched for our unfinished cigars, but the donkeys already ate them. Another day, another dollar cigar.

"Rollin, Rollin, Rollin, keep them donkeys movin..."

## LAND OF THE '59ers
### Summer 1996, San Juan Mountains, Colorado

The flyer I tacked on the mining museum bulletin board read: *Welcome to Lake City Colorado! Land of HISTORIC ROARING BOOMTOWN MINING CAMPS! The HARD TACK MINING COMPANY is taking tour groups through an HISTORIC SILVER MINE! Walk deep into the side of a mountain and see veins of SILVER! Watch for initials and graffiti old timers left on the tunnel walls by using their carbide lights. Listen for the sound of Tommyknockers. Legend says if you leave them a little food it is good luck.*

*Find SILVER ORE! Hard hats and miners lights provided...*

Our mission in life, this summer anyway, was conducting underground mine tours and hauling silver ore (galena) from other tunnels and mine dumps that intersected the same vein, then salt the tour tunnel and sell specimens.

The California mine tunnel used for tours, had a stoped out area, sometimes called a raise, over forty feet high and two hundred feet long, a cathedral size multi-level room at the end of a long drift.

George, the mine owner said, "Can't blast during tourist season, leaves the tunnel kinda stinky. Nope too risky. I'll get my powder monkey out this winter, we'll blast to the upper level and drop lots more rock. The best ore mined last winter sure got picked over fast! You and the burros can haul some ore from the Hidden Treasure Mine. Good stuff piled all over up there. Same ore, same vein. Hard to get to though!"

The San Juan Mountains, the largest most mineralized range in Colorado, contains hundreds of summits over thirteen thousand feet. One fourth of all the peaks in North America over fourteen thousand feet are here in some of the most wildly rugged mountains in the world!

Deep canyons and perpendicular rock walls serrated with quartz veins rise 1,200 to 1,500 feet.

We camped at the Hard Tack Mine, a short walk from the ghost town of Henson. Elevation 9,200 feet. Within a few miles radius were about three hundred old hard rock mine workings and a score of ghost towns and mining camps.

Also nearby was the massacre site and monument to the victims of Alferd Packer "the human cannibal." According to newspaper and trial accounts, in 1874 Alferd guided five prospectors over the mountains, although Packer knew little of the rugged San Juans.

Winter came and it was discovered that Alferd despite claims of starvation was well fleshed out and had a great deal of money. The prospectors bodies were found with blocks of flesh carved out in an unnatural manner. This old news item is Lake City's morbid joke. There is Cannibal Outdoors Outfitters and Guide Service,

Alferd Packer Days festivities, and Alferd Packer cookbooks. (The spelling, Alferd instead of Alfred, was preferred by Packer.)

By a steep game trail, once a wagon road, we hauled ore from the Hidden Treasure mine dump site, one thousand feet above base camp with our donkey pack string. Mud, snow, and rock slides have buried many roads, towns, and mines (including this road) in these precipitous mountains.

One day while climbing the trail for a load of ore, a talus slide started above us.

Mike yelled, "Look up there! A lynx!"

I looked, but the cat was gone. The moving rocks sounded like a dump truck load of broken glass. I couldn't believe a small silent, usually nocturnal cat could dislodge a landslide, but something did.

The rock slide startled Sarah and she stepped back off the trail, tumbled, and skidded down the tinkling scree bank below us. Her legs tangled in the break away lead rope, the breeching ripped, and the rear cinch dragged behind her.

Mike jumped after her and glided like a surfer on a wave of rocks and cut her rigging with a knife. Both still sliding.

I had my camera poised, but did not have the nerve of a reporter to take pictures with captions that might read, "Last time I saw Sarah and Mike alive was . . . "

But they finally stopped and Mike yelled, "Don't stand there with your mouth open, throw me some line! So I hooked three picket lines together and Mike tied the panniers and packsaddle to the line. Mike traversed the hill to some aspen trees and Sarah slid further down the slope and regained her footing. We pulled the gear up after all the animals were clear of the slide area and took inventory, a few broken straps, and a cracked water can. Lucky.

We reloaded the donkeys with the extra gear and headed back to camp. This ore shipment would have to wait.

We found Sarah grazing near camp, unflustered. She swished her tail and brayed as if to say, "What took you guys so long anyway?"

## MOOSE, MOSQUITOS, AND GOLD

Hauling silver ore and working cool damp mine tunnels during the hot summer in Colorado was great, but we missed finding gold so we set up our new high-banker in the donkey water trough and re-ran our Idaho gold over the riffles. Then we panned and re-panned the same gold. "Gee, ain't it purty!" This was quite fun and we sold panning lessons in the process. The donkeys would drink from their trough while we panned and drip water on our heads. We didn't mind this, in fact tourists thought it entertaining, but Willy went too far one day when he slurped all the water from my gold pan and licked up the black sand and gold. I got to pan for lost gold the next day in donkey tailings.

The gold we panned here in the land of silver was from Florence, Idaho; a mining district we renamed "Little Alaska" . . . marshes, moose, mosquitoes, gold!

Central Idaho has impressive metallic ore deposits, and those deposits concentrate around the margins of the Idaho Batholith; at the southwest edge is Florence. This district has extensive glacial deposits. Two to four feet below the surface looks like river rock mixed with ground and broken granite and quartz—and a rust seam in places. These rusty bands in the gravel held the coarse gold and small nuggets. Our donkeys hauled five gallon buckets of paydirt over their wood frame sawbuck packsaddles to our sluice set up on Meadow Creek.

Morning and evening we saw a cow and calf and a young bull moose, and every other day the old bull. Sometimes a giant, ugly, grouchy, hunchback, barren cow moose lurked around and charged the bulls.

When she bristled her nape hair, she looked eight feet tall. The young bull moose we named "Bullwinkle." He browsed, pulling up greens from the creek bottom.

He would stroll by two or three times a day, even if we set up our tents miles from base camp. I think he had a crush on our jennets, Sarah and Lacey.

An old timer up here said, "Sometimes them moose bulls get in love with a rancher's beef cow. Gives a new meaning to the word 'MOOOOOOOSE'."

One evening as Bullwinkle grazed in the creek near our camp, the ill-humored old cow moose charged the young bull. Bullwinkle rose dripping from the creek and hit our single strand polywire donkey fence. The polywire got wrapped around his hind legs and he dragged the whole fence, plastic posts and all. The donkeys calmly wandered off grazing (except Willy the gray gelding) while Bullwinkle headed toward us, away from the cow.

The bull looked bigger up close—our rifle thirty feet away, pistol in the tent. So Mike banged on pans and I grabbed Willy by the halter.

Willy snorted, stomped, and tried to challenge the moose. "Dammit Willy," I said, "you're like a Pekinese barking at a freight train!"

Bullwinkle turned and trotted away pulling five hundred feet of polywire behind him. The wire eventually slid off his hind legs and we retrieved our portable fence.

We caught the other donkeys, then ate dinner.

"That was exciting," Mike said, "but just wait till rutting season starts."

## A PROSPECTOR'S FRIEND

On a street in Fairplay, Colorado is a small stone monument to a prospector's partner, and a bronze picture of Prunes a burro. Rupe his owner considered Prunes his best friend and named him for his prune color and love of the dried fruit. A good prospector always shared food with his working partner.

Rupe and Prunes prospected the Alma Fairplay mining district for fifty years. Prunes was 63 years old when he died. Before Rupe died a year later he requested his ashes be placed next to his burro. Rupe was 80 years old.

Klondike Mike and I looked at each other and exclaimed, "63 YEARS OLD!"

"Geez" I said "I didn't know those rascals could live that long?"

We met Dick, the Grand Canyon jack before he died. He was 40 years old and just sired two burritos. A fellow in Idaho had a 45 year old gelding. He soaked the donkey's alfalfa pellets and hay cubes, "Cause the old boy ain't got enough teeth left to eat hay and stuff proper like."

We expected 40 to 45 year life spans from our donks, but sixty? "By God" Mike said "our donkeys will out live us!"

"And," I replied, "I guess we'll be putting up with their antics for a long time . . . Remember when we were north of Silver City near Mogollon?"

We had ridden to a frontier mine dump. I unsaddled Shaggy and Sarah and put them on thirty foot tethers. Mike took the wood panniers and packsaddles off Willy and Lacey and released the two.

The metal detectors were in the panniers. We unwrapped them, snapped them together, did some fine tuning, and set out to treasure hunt.

Mike headed down the ravine to the base of the mine dump with the Falcon probe, a rock hammer, chisel, and ore sample bags. I stayed near the mine tunnel and the browsing donkeys. This area has quartz crystals, fluorite, pyrite, lead and silver galena, gem grade chrysocolla, and if we're lucky gold. I cracked rocks and put interesting heavy samples of rust and black colored minerals in my ore bags—found some crystals, two old mule shoes, and a cute little well worn donkey shoe. We didn't have to shoe our donkeys because they're not used for heavy road or mine work. Donkeys have a rubbery hoof, much like a goat and are more sure footed without metal shoes.

Willy the gray gelding was a pest that day. He pulled the canvas flaps on the panniers trying to get the snacks, then scattered the bridles, ropes, and blankets and pestered the other donkeys who were busy munching brush.

He came up behind me and snatched the straw hat off my head and pranced off hoping I'd chase him, which I usually did, but this time I was busy on hands and knees digging out a spot below a promising beep.

Willy came back and gave me a hard shove with his nose then grabbed the sling attached to my metal detector. He pranced off again, the metal detector's plastic disc dragging over rocks to staccato beeps and clunks.

"WILLY STOP! YOU DARN JACKASS, GET BACK HERE!"

That didn't work so I walked slowly toward him and tried my serious patient voice, "Whoa, Willy, whoa. Steady boy, steady." He thought this quite a fun game as I heard the scrape and clatter of my precious metal detector. But a sharp high pitched screech from the black box caused Willy to drop it. He jumped back, spun in a circle, stared and brayed at the screaming object.

"Well I'll be Willy, you found something!" I dug furiously, sure it was a huge nugget found by MY jackass. We'd be famous, "Largest nugget ever found in the Mogollon Mining District." But it was a rusted steel ball about four and a half inches in diameter. Maybe from a ball mill, or a small cannon? Not gold but the momentary adrenalin rush kept the hunt exciting.

I decided to tie Willy and see if the Gold Bug metal detector was still OK. I had to retune it. Besides a few nicks and scrapes it was fine. Now my detector had the well used look of a "professional" treasure hunter's tool.

I walked over to Willy and scratched his neck and back. His lower lip drooped and his eyelids closed.

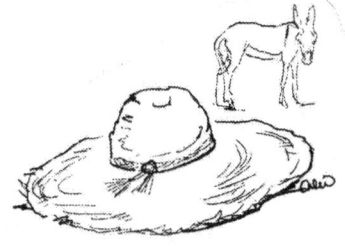

Donkeys live to be how old?

## NEW MEXICO OR BUST!
### Fall

Uncle Wayne sent a message via the Forest Service folks: "Silver mine and ghost town for sale in southwest New Mexico, go check it out. Enclosed is a map, some names and addresses, and a cashier's check. Uncle Wayne."

"YIPEE!" I screeched and danced, "YIPEE! MIKE! MIKE! GUESS WHAT? GUESS WHAT?"

"Oh no, now what," Mike said, "is Wayne sending us to the Congo or something?"

"No, not quite, but close to the Mexico border. Here's the map and stuff."

Mike looked at the money and yelled, "YA HOO!" We hugged and danced.

"This is great! On the edge of a new adventure, a new mission in life! And," I said, "just because we are looking at a silver mine, doesn't mean we can't hunt for gold on the journey south. Besides that it's still probably one-hundred plus degrees down there."

Mike found the *Guide To Gold In New Mexico* and planned our route from Colorado. He said, "Load em up! Move em out! First stop, Placer Creek, east of the Rio Brazos."

I looked at the topo map. "Good God Mike, Placer Creek is ten thousand feet above sea level. I hope it doesn't snow."

The bunch grass was sparse, but knee high. The weather cool and sunny. We saddled and packed the donkeys and prospected upstream and downstream. After days of sampling and panning we found flakes of rough gold.

"Finally," I said, "but of course the best gold is in the steepest most narrow part of the entire canyon . . . Uh, oh! Mike, look at those big black clouds, damn!"

It snowed and snowed and the wind blew and blew, sending us and our donkey overloaded fifth-wheel trailer to a lower elevation. Next stop, the ghost town of Rosedale in the San Mateo Mountains near Magdalena, only 7,200 feet above sea level, warm and sunny, good grazing, and lots of promising gold mine dumps.

"Jill, look to the north, big black clouds."

"Oh no, not again!" Hard freezing rain pelted and burned our faces, and the wind blew and blew, so we loaded the herd and headed south. The blizzard pushed us to the Peloncillo Mountains (only 4,600 feet elevation) near Mexico and Uncle Wayne's new prospect.

The temperature here was in the upper 90's. I said, "Well, at least it's not snowing."

Anxious to explore the old mining camp, we put the packsaddles and panniers on Willy and Shaggy. Sarah and Lacey stayed in camp with their new foals. Hard hats, flashlights, extra batteries, hammer, pick, shovel, ax, machete, ore sacks, canteens, candles . . .

The steep old wagon road, now an obscure trail to the first mine tunnel was thick with five foot high prickly pear, ocotillo, cholla, and mesquite. We skirted boulders which blocked parts of this hand built 1880s rock road and had to unload the donkeys twice to get through.

"Geez Mike, it took us two hours to ascend 400 feet, are we getting old or what?"

"Nope," Mike said, "just don't want to get prickly peared."

At the mine portal we removed the panniers from Shag and Willy—loosened their cinches and tied them to the old twisted ore car track that jutted from the tunnel.

The tunnel entrance only four feet high, so stooping we moved slowly to let our eyes adjust from bright sunlight to the dimness of our flashlights.

I remarked, "There's a nice breeze, good sign, good air." After crouching about 300 feet, the tunnel opened to raises and natural caverns, filled with white calcite and crystal vugs.

Mike said, "Should have brought our ultra-violet lamps, probably lots of fluorescent stuff here."

We explored dead end drifts that branched off the main tunnel. "This is sure dry and dusty compared to the damp dripping tunnels up north. Uncle Wayne said to watch for denning rattlesnakes. He said snakes have a distinct cucumber odor. I don't smell anything. Do you?"

"No Jill, we're probably too far back for snakes. Hopefully. Well anyway, the tunnel looks safe and solid, let's keep going."

We passed what looked like shafts filled with waste rock. Mike commented, "Was easier than hauling muck all the way to the tunnel entrance."

"So this," I said, "is what Uncle Wayne calls rat hole mining." The drifts followed veins left, right, up, and down. The low cramped tunnels twisted and turned, unlike spacious modern mine tunnels, engineered for mucking machines and equipment the size of dump trucks.

In a pile of tobacco cans and smashed buckets was an unusual looking candle holder made from a donkey shoe. I put it in my ore sack. Deeper into the mountain we followed ore car tracks.

Around the next bend Mike found a half buried kerosene lamp—glass broken. Then on a metal rod supported by a beam was mummified ribs and leg bones. I gasped, "What the hell is this?"

We crept forward certain to meet a grinning skull or ghosts of the murdered pelting rocks on our head and cursing us for entering their haunted sanctuary. But when we got nearer the hanging bones and dried flesh we noticed bovine looking hooves. At the end of one backbone was a tail with a tuft of brown and white hair.

I said, "Beef quarters. Really, really old beef quarters."

"Wow," Mike said, "cattle rustlers! Wayne will get a kick out of this. I guess a cattle thief hauled beef back here where it's cool and no flies. Even the coyotes didn't come back this far."

"Mike it's dried hard like a piece of wood." So we tapped on it. "Let's leave it here, might make an interesting exhibit. Must be 100 years old!"

According to locals Granite Gap Mine lay at the fork of Cowboy Pass Trail, and Granite Gap Pass, a frontier stage and wagon road.

The Clanton Gang hung around here sometimes, Pancho Villa, and other Mexican and gringo banditos and cattle rustlers used this trail. The town and roads pushed into Apache territory, and some lost treasure books mention the Granite Gap stagecoach robbery and buried gold bars.

"Dear Uncle Wayne. The ghost town of Granite Gap is piles of rusty cans, acres of broken glass and rotten wood. Remnants of miners cave camps and rock cabins. Miles of tunnels in granite and limestone. Some tunnels have six levels and go all the way through the mountain. We found silver lead galena, smithsonite, hemimorphite, chrysocolla, aurichalcite, malachite... We think you should buy it. P.S. Uncle Wayne do you want partners on this venture?"

## CIGARS AND BLACK GOLD
### Winter, Granite Gap Mine & Peloncillo Mountains

A familiar old truck rattled into base camp and slid to a stop almost hitting our wobbly legged table. The wind whipped dust into our eyes and the truck horn blasted in my left ear, then the donkeys started braying near my right ear. The peace of the day was over.

Uncle Wayne drove from the northern border of the "lower 48" (which he informed us was under three feet of snow) and arrived here near Mexico, the southern border of the lower 48.

Klondike Mike informed Uncle Wayne, "Been sixty to seventy degrees most days." Although we failed to mention the seventy-five mile per hour gust of wind that blew the roof off the donkey shed; we'd tell him later.

Uncle Wayne wore a Cheshire cat grin. "Did you strike it rich or something?" Mike asked. Uncle Wayne stood there still grinning; it was irritating.

"OK, OK. Uncle Wayne," I said impatiently, "You either have twelve cases of white lightning or a couple pounds of gold. So what is it? C'mon spill the beans."

Uncle Wayne reached into his truck and handed Mike and I each a fat cigar that looked a foot long.

"This smells like a twenty dollar seegar." Mike remarked. "Did you have a baby or did all your cows have calves?"

I snorted.

Uncle Wayne lit his cigar, and I got him a cup of coffee. We sat down at the flimsy table. Maybe now he'd talk.

"We had lots of rain this summer up in the Okanogan Highlands, and good snow pack. The creek ran strong until September; welded up a hell of a sluice." Uncle Wayne paused, took a few sips of lukewarm coffee and puffed on his cigar. "Me and the old mules, we decided to semi-retire, so I bought me a backhoe and diverted the creek just a wee bit."

I gasped and choked on the coffee I was sipping. I knew if Uncle Wayne diverted his creek a "wee bit" it meant the creek now ran into the next canyon. "Good grief Uncle Wayne!" I said, "I hope you routed it back before you left; wouldn't want the EPA swat team to rape and pillage your humble estate."

Uncle Wayne spat a piece of cigar butt on the ground and said, "Naturally."

Wayne walked to his rusted truck and pulled out a dented metal tackle box wrapped with a bungee cord and decorated with silver duct tape which served as a hinge.

I laughed. "Looks like that thing bounced down the walls of the Grand Canyon; or did one of your mules stomp it."

"Naw," Mike teased, "he found buried treasure."

Uncle Wayne ignored us and with a flourish unhooked the bungee cord and flopped back the dirty duct taped hinged lid. Mike's mouth dropped open and my eyes bugged out. Little rows of one ounce gold vials glowed from the battered tray. Most of it was flour gold, very fine, but a few vials had smooth clinkers.

In the bottom of the tackle box Wayne had an egg carton base. Each foam nest held either an off-white or a dull gray granitic looking rock. Uncle Wayne took out a gray rock. It had little black lines and specks. I held it. Heavy. Mike examined it.

I said, "No offense, Uncle Wayne, it's ugly." Then Wayne handed me an off-white rock. Little strings and specks of gold. Gorgeous!

Uncle Wayne said, "Both these rocks are the same ore from the same dump. I heated these in a forge." He pointed to the light colored rocks with the visible gold strings. "These other rocks with the black lines haven't been roasted yet. Black gold, gold telluride." Uncle Wayne shouted and laughed, "FIRE AND BRIMSTONE!"

Mike asked, "Where'd you get all this?"

Wayne said, "The flour I got at my place. Used the backhoe and the newly carpeted sluice, worked real good. The clinkers I traded for, and the gold ore I found on my way north last spring in Colorado; some claims up there for sale, under ten feet of snow now. I thought maybe this summer, you and Mike and the donkeys could go up and—"

I interrupted, "Forget it Uncle Wayne, I don't want to be stuck at twelve thousand feet elevation, sliding down canyons, having heart attacks, and it takes two weeks to properly cook a pot of beans! While YOU spend YOUR summers at a comfortable four thousand feet near the Canadian border using a backhoe. Like last summer, dammit! I just about died down here! A hundred and twenty damn degrees in the shade! No power! Thirty four miles round trip for water!"

"But," Uncle Wayne said, "there's plenty of water in Colorado."

I jumped up so fast my aluminum lawn chair fell over and collapsed, I grabbed my cholla walking stick and chased Uncle Wayne around his truck. He was too spry and quick for me. Shaggy and Willy started braying, they loved a good game of chase.

Uncle Wayne yelled, "Mike. Help! Save me from this violent woman!"

Then Mike chased me brandishing a vulture feather he had found.

The donkeys used this opportunity and wandered to the unguarded table and munched leftovers. Shaggy stood at the table eating crackers and in Willy's donkey lips a foot long cigar dangled. We all laughed so hard we couldn't stand. Mike and Wayne clutched the truck bed and gasped for air. I fell to the ground, held my stomach and peed my pants.

## MOUNTAIN LIONS AND BIGHORN SHEEP
### Spring, Peloncillo Mountains

Uncle Wayne was arguing with Klondike Mike near a newly acquired stack of old lumber, the soon to be rock shop and trading post.

Uncle Wayne said, "We don't need no fancy dry goods, just maybe tobacco, flour, axle grease, salt, and beans. A respectable line of frontier groceries."

Mike said rather loudly, "That's ridiculous! We don't even have enough wood to build a floor, and there is no glass for the windows. The flour and the beans will just get bug infested! Besides that nobody buys that kind of stuff anymore."

Uncle Wayne said, "But we do!"

Mike replied, "But we ain't exactly normal."

Uncle Wayne pondered this for awhile and said, "Why don't we fill empty flour sacks with lime or something and bean sacks with rocks. That will give the store an authentic Old West look."

While they argued I put the McClellan cavalry saddle on Willy and the sawbuck packsaddle and wood panniers on Shag. I planned to rummage around the ghost mining camp and a couple of mine dumps for saleable items.

From the surrounding flat country where the Chihuahuan Desert overlaps the Sonoran Desert spectacular granite and limestone ridges and rock formations rise up all around us.

The donkeys radar ears pointed to a place in the columns of rocks above us. The desert bighorn sheep moved down the mountain. Their hooves clicked softly on the granite boulders that looked like weathered and eroded giants turned to stone. We all watched the wild sheep for awhile. (The donkeys often watched distant moving specks. Sometimes they heard movement beyond 10X binocular range.)

I tied Shag to Willy's saddle and put my foot in the stirrup and began to swing my leg over but the saddle slipped sideways and I flopped grunting under Willy. Shag sniffed me and Willy turned his head and stared at me and I noted a gleam in his eye. I forgot to retighten the saddle after he puffed himself up like a blow fish when I first cinched him up. Good thing Uncle Wayne and Mike were now debating where to build the store, so they didn't see me sprawled, backside, hat, and hair covered with sand. Their preoccupation with the pile of old wood saved me endless guffaws.

The townsite was less than a half mile away, but hauling back stove parts, beer buckets, glass bottles, horse and donkey shoes, silver ore, and beautiful blue copper ore was usually easier with the donkeys.

Granite Gap New Mexico is dry, dusty, prickly, nostalgic. Scattered tin, broken bottles, rust, crumbled wood, junk heaps . . . Over a century ago the tent and poorly built adobe and rock town had saloons, sporting houses, trading posts, a livery stable, church, school, jail, and assay office.

Mens' hammers on drill steel, the rumble of blasting deep in the mountain, the clank of shod horses on stone, and sometimes at night the sound of a harmonica. Water $1 a barrel. Baths 25 cents. The lukewarm bathwater always gray and greasy. You had to scoop off the drowned centipedes, wasps, moths, tarantulas, and occasional dead mouse before stepping in. A quiet town, no shoot-outs, only men too tired to fight.

Local history claims 500 people lived here at the height of the silver boom in the late 1800s. The population at its peak was most likely closer to 300, if that.

Every former mining town boasts their town was the wildest, meanest, biggest, and toughest of all. This is truth-stretching (as Huck Finn called it) typical of ghost town histories. We brag about the lawless behavior of our ancestors. This is known as color. Fighting, robbery, murder, and lynchings are what is called the colorful past. Although I doubt this bragged about colorfulness was enjoyable at the time.

A Colorado historian said, "Only Engineer City, atop Engineer Pass 13,000 feet elevation claimed to be the only town in the West with not one saloon or sporting establishment!"

I replied, "After my experience working up there I suspect most miners and engineers were too altitude sick to hang out at a saloon or sporting house. They just wanted to 'Get the hell down off this mountain.'" These miners sought entertainment elsewhere.

The town of Granite Gap fell into oblivion, no boothill, just scattered grave sites located near loose moveable rocks. The land here is solid bedrock; rather than waste man power and powder to blast holes, rocks were piled hastily over the canvas wrapped corpse (as buzzards circled above and the heat made the carcass stink). Wood much too scarce to build coffins.

The livery stable was a ramada made of yucca stalks and mesquite. The big horses that could reach ate the yucca roof. Spiny ocotillo called coachwhip was planted and woven between scraps of wood for a corral. Rocks were piled around fence posts to hold them somewhat upright. The burros ate most of the ocotillo leaves that dared grow into the corral. The gate was two broken wagon wheels wired and propped up, sometimes they fell over. The toothless livery man dribbling tobacco juice would cuss a blue streak when all the stock wandered off. Jezebel the town's pet burro was usually the culprit. She could untie knots and open latches, and often wandered town, entering tents and adobe houses begging for bread and a bucket of beer.

The old saddle creaked under me, the donkeys clip-clopped through town. I imagined it was 1882 and I brought in silver and turquoise for supplies. The scale sat on the rough wood counter, a dusty, crowded dim-lit store . . .

Suddenly I was snapped out of my reverie. Nine bighorn sheep stampeded off the granite boulders into the ravine behind us. Willy bolted and snapped Shag's lead and began to buck. I was thrown hard on a pile of rocks. I gasped for breath.

Willy and Shag stopped about thirty feet from where I lay groaning. Willy stomped and snorted. Both sets of donkey ears pointed to a ridge above us. There strolling casually were two mountain lions. Possibly a female with a yearling cub.

The two big cats glanced at us, their glinting yellow eyes, indifferent. They turned and moved silently, deep into the hoodoo rock formations.

I couldn't get up. It felt like my bones fused into the rock. "Willy, Shaggy, get over here. Help me." But they were too busy

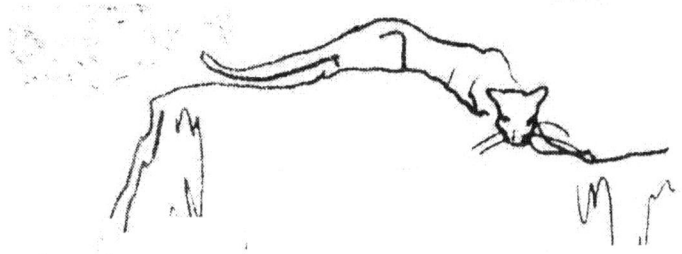

staring after the lions. I fumbled through my pockets and found a well worn pack of Levi Garrett chewing tobacco. The donkeys heard the familiar crinkle of foil paper and their huge ears turned my way. Chewing tobacco is donkey candy. They daintily stepped toward me over the rocks. Soon I had eager donkey heads hanging over me. I fed them the rest of the tobacco and pulled myself up, weak and shaky, using a stirrup on Willy's saddle. Mounting was impossible, so I found a stick to use like a cane and hobbled back to camp. I removed Willy's bridle, draped it over his saddle and I told the boys to go on home, but instead they escorted me while they browsed on bunch grass and brush, in no hurry.

I was not anxious to get back to camp. I knew exactly what Uncle Wayne would say, "Should've paid attention, been alert. No adult should ever get bucked off a donkey..."

I limped into camp. Mike asked, "What happened to you?"

I said, "Willy bucked me off, mountain lions scared him."

Uncle Wayne commented, "Never should have got bucked off a donkey, you weren't paying attention, you should have..."

I looked at Uncle Wayne and crossed my eyes, turned and hobbled toward the tent where my cot and soft foam pad waited. Mike unsaddled, brushed, and fed the donkeys. Uncle Wayne was still talking about the proper way to stay mounted on a bucking bronco as he waved a half finished tuna sandwich in the air. The only one interested in Uncle Wayne's lecture and gestures was Tilly the Hun, Uncle Wayne's new cat.

## LOCOWEED
### Granite Gap

The little pony stumbled around camp looking for handouts, dazed, senile. I asked Jake the rancher, "Who owns that pony? What's wrong with him?"

Jake said, "Don't know, just showed up on the range one day. We let him be—probably got into locoweed, he'll never be right again."

"Oh," I said, "we feed him soaked grain and alfalfa pellets. Sometimes he can't hardly chew or swallow."

Jake leaned against his pickup truck, tilted back his ancient Stetson, "If you want to waste your time and money that's your business. Found any gold or buried treasure yet?"

"Me and Mike found some old worn down coins, bottles, and three arrowheads."

"Yep," Jake said, "lots of arrowheads around here, some Apache, some older. Well, I gotta go." Jake got into his truck and rattled down the road to check on his cattle.

Two weeks later we found the pony dead under his favorite

mesquite tree. I said sadly, "I hope we made his last days comfortable as we could. Anyway if he had to die this is good a place as any. The carcass should give us some good observations on scavengers. Maybe I can sell an article to *Southwest Carnivore Magazine*."

Mike gave me a disgusted look, said nothing, turned and walked away. Well, darn I liked the pony too, but the donkeys didn't miss him, especially Willy who was jealous and irritated with the drunk-acting equine.

As it turned out a local biologist named Sandilee said, "I'll pay you one-hundred fifty dollars to take photos and make track castings of the animals that visit the carcass." She packs a pistol, eats rattlesnake meat, and cusses out endangered species activists, "A bunch of damn city dwellers that fly over in helicopters once in a while and make trouble for us! But, anyway we can all make money this summer collecting snakes and poisonous insects and spiders for venom research."

"Ha, Ha!" I said, "Who says we can't earn money prospecting? We just have to be flexible."

Actually our funds were running low. The holiday months, a slow time of year for the panning booth, donkey rides, mineral sales, and mine tours.

"Mike we may have to temporarily bid farewell to our glorious freedom and enter a self-imposed jail sentence, and get jobs."

I remembered the countless times I was encouraged to get a good civil service "job."

"But why," I'd say, "should I have a normal steady job doing work I don't want to do in order to live a way I don't want to live?"

Over twenty years ago I bought forty acres with a neat liveable cave in the Okanogan Highlands, only fifty bucks a month and I got a "job" flipping burgers during the tourist season at the Wauconda Café, worked for the Forest Service, and mined in Alaska. Not much has changed. As Edward Abbey wrote, "Survival with honor."

We sold specimens of rhodochrosite, smithsonite and other valuable minerals to collectors and dealers. Bought and sold some donkeys, and got paid to tear down a couple of old buildings and haul them away. Not real jobs, but gainfully self-unemployed.

One of our friends, a Hidalgo County Deputy Sheriff stopped by to visit. Glenn showed us the gold he panned on Turkey Creek. Our hard rock mines had silver and rare minerals, but so far no gold.

"Uncle Wayne will you watch the mine for a week or so while we go on a quest? We need to replenish the panning booth gold. We're still selling gold from Idaho." I said.

"We could buy a few ounces of gold for spot price."

"But Uncle Wayne that's obscene, that's cheating!"

Uncle Wayne chuckled and walked away and yelled back, "See you in a week or two."

We loaded the truck and stock trailer; Shaggy, Willy, packsaddles, panniers, tent, sluice, gold pans . . .

"Mike is this considered a job? Are we gainfully employed?"

"Nope, it's not a real job unless you can collect unemployment money."

"Oh." I said. "Well donkeys are you ready to go?"

They brayed lustily as if to say, "Quit yakking and let's get going, we have a 'job' to do."

## TOMMYKNOCKERS

### Gila National Forest, New Mexico

The fire crackled, the glow danced on the rock walls casting eerie shadows. Uncle Wayne in a scary whisper said, "Knock! Knock! Tap! Tap! What's that sound? Tis the sound of a Tommyknocker here underground. Knock! Knock! Tap! Tap! Who goes there? It's a Tommyknocker, knocking on the midnight air. The sound of his tapping will serve no doubt, To warn us miners, That we better GET OUT!" Uncle Wayne lept up and roared like a bear, my nephews screamed in delighted fright.

While the storm raged outside, we huddled close to the comforting fire, listening.

The morning started out a typical clear, sunny fall day. A perfect time to teach the boys about metal detecting. While nugget shooting Uncle Wayne and Lane found a couple of clinkers. Klondike Mike rolled over some boulders and dug a few holes in the sand down to bedrock, good spots to check for gold.

Mike said, "This place is always too dry to dredge, and too wet for dry washing. A high-banker with re-circulating water would work. Hey, you donkeys! Did you hear that? Next time you'll have to haul extra water too!" Willy and Shaggy flicked their tails and gave Mike a sullen look.

We listened, intent to the beeping of our finely tuned instruments; so obsessed in finding more gold, we didn't pay attention to the drop in temperature, the wind change, and the donkeys odd behavior. Shaggy and Willy tossed their heads, pawed the ground, stomped. Their huge ears pointed westward. Willy trotted in circles, and both donkeys began to bray; a sharp, staccato, "danger is near" bray.

I called out, "Mike, Wayne, something is wrong! Look at the donkeys!"

Uncle Wayne watched and listened for a moment, then looked west and yelled, "GET OUT OF THIS GULCH! GET OUT OF THIS GULCH! NOW!"

Mike clutched Lane and Evan by their arms and hurried uphill. Uncle Wayne gathered the metal detectors, shovels, and pick, while I quickly slung the pannier boxes on Willy's and Shaggy's packsaddles and stuffed everything strewn on the ground into the packs.

Then it happened. Huge rolling black clouds blotted out the sun. A gust of wind blew ice cold. The sleet drove into my face while I stumbled and scrambled upward. The donkeys pressed close behind me. I heard rumbling like the sound of an avalanche. I turned and looked down where we all stood moments ago, a river of mud, rocks and small trees crashed down Gold Gulch.

The sleet turned into pounding rain and I started slipping. Mike grabbed Shaggy's lead, so I grasped a leather strap on Willy's lopsided pack and held on. He pulled me up the slick mud bank to the tunnel entrance.

Gasping I said, "Thank God for old mines."

Mike added, "And smart donkeys."

We unloaded the donkeys and took off their packsaddles. Everything and everybody dripped puddles of water onto the powder dry floor.

"Yuk," Evan said, "we need to build a fire." So we found the flashlights, and crept deeper into the tunnel. A light warm breeze, and solid rock walls, a good sign. About two hundred feet inside we found an air shaft and remains of an ore chute. We could use this wood for a fire.

The boys and I went back to feed, water, and praise the donkeys; then carry soggy supplies and sleeping bags to the underground campsite. I lashed a line to some boulders across the tunnel entrance. I told my nephews, "The rope is there just in case the weather clears, then Shag and Willy won't wander off. The donkeys can follow us to the campfire, sometimes they do, but they'll probably munch barley and watch the storm from their secure hideaway. Sort of like eating popcorn and watching TV."

We sat close to the fire. Uncle Wayne said, "That was a gully washer you boys saw, a real turd floater. The donkeys saved all our stuff, maybe even our lives."

Lane exclaimed, "Wow! Really?"

"Yep," Uncle Wayne said, "and there are other creatures or beings that saved many miners' lives. One is the Tommyknocker. Some say they are ghosts, and some say they are spirits of dead miners. But the Cornishmen know they're kin to the elves and sprites of Cornwall, brought here with the Cornish miners.

"Legend claims their origin goes back to some ancient forgotten race forced by the first Celt invasions to hide in the moorlands and the cliffs.

"When the Knackers crossed the Atlantic and became Tommyknockers they were regarded with deep affection by the Cornishmen who worked in these dark and narrow stopes." Wayne looked up and pointed, "Boys see that platform way up there?

The miners stood and drilled holes in the rock standing on that platform.

"Many a miner told stories about hearing loud persistent knock-knocking, then he'd put down his tools and say, 'This hole is deep enough!' and hurried out, but before he reached the surface a cave-in happened at the stope he'd just left.

"Wise miners always left a piece of bread or a bite of food, to keep on the sprites good side. They were friendly little fellows who liked to play tricks. Sometimes they would hide a miner's pick and shovel or upset his lunch bucket.

"I worked in a gold mine near British Columbia, while drilling a hole overhead, something pushed me hard into the adjoining drift tunnel. Then with a thud, a huge boulder fell right where I was drilling. A Tommyknocker saved my life."

Evan asked, "Did you see him?"

We sat silent waiting for Wayne to reply. He began to speak when we heard, tap-tap, tap-tap. We stared at each other bug-eyed. Uncle Wayne answered with a tap-tap, tap-tap. The distant tapping came nearer, then it stopped.

Uncle Wayne stretched and yawned, "We have donkey guards at the entrance and Tommyknocker guards to our rear, we are quite secure. Goodnight everyone."

None of us slept soundly except Uncle Wayne, who snored loud, totally relaxed.

## LADRONE

*Let me now with my donkey tread again upon plain ground, . . . let everyone stick to the calling he was born to.*

— **Sancho Panza from *Don Quixote***

The donkey (or burro) worked the mines and carried the prospectors tools, bedroll, beans, and bacon. On his packsaddle hung a water canteen, an empty lard bucket which served as a coffee pot, and a skillet for frying rabbit, bacon, or venison.

If the prospector was a placer miner, the skillet also served as a gold pan. Many gold strikes were made panning with skillets, wood bowls, tin plates, or tin cups.

In his search for precious metals the prospector penetrated isolated and treacherous regions with only his donkey as a companion.

These frontier prospectors often sold their mining claims cheap, not interested in settling down and developing their discoveries. Instead the prospector bought more supplies, loaded his donkey and left town for the beckoning mountains and deserts.

A donkey named Jack owned by Mr. O. Peck wandered untethered and foraged for himself. Two prospectors, Noah Kellogg and Phillip O'Rourke, came upon the friendly donkey and took him. Later while pawing the ground for roots or a place to roll, Jack uncovered a rich outcrop of silver ore which became the Bunker Hill and Sullivan mines of Idaho. The legal owner of the donkey, Mr. Peck, claimed that because of his donkey's part in the discovery of the rich silver strike, he was due royalties. The Supreme Court of Idaho agreed: "This court is of the opinion that the Bunker Hill mine was discovered by Peck's burro. Phillip O'Rourke, and N.S. Kellogg, and, therefore, he [Peck] is entitled to one-third interest in the property." At the time of the court's decision the property was valued at fifteen million dollars.

In another court case, the lawyer for the defense in his effort to qualify his witness as an expert asked how long he had been a prospector. The prospector replied, "For thirty years."

When the attorney for the prosecution questioned the witness, the prospector replied, "Well I really only prospected for five years." The prosecutor believing he had trapped the witness pointed out the discrepancy. But the prospector countered, "I've prospected for five years and spent the other twenty-five looking for my burros." The judge accepted him as a witness.

James A. McKenna, a prospector who collected tales of the Black Range in New Mexico, was impressed with the burro's inquisitiveness: "All burros have a regular human lump of curiosity. They like to hang around the new mining camps. I have seen as many as twenty burros standing in front of a dance hall, or watching a big faro game, just as close to the door as they could get and as silent as ghosts."

McKenna also told the story of a burro named Ladrone (Spanish for "thief"). Ladrone was wandering the Black Range country. Two brothers, Joe and Jim Hyatt "adopted" him. One day while the Hyatts were in the hills prospecting, a sow bear with cubs attacked them. Ladrone chased the cubs and diverted the raging bear's attention from the Hyatt boys.

Nicholas Creede and his donkey searched twenty years for gold, from the Mexican to Canadian borders. Finally in 1890, Creede made his strike. Creede, Colorado bears his name today. In its mining heyday it was a prosperous, boisterous town. Cy Warman the town newspaper owner wrote:

> *Here the meek and mild-eyed burros*
> *On mineral mountain feed*
> *It's day all day in the daytime*
> *And there is no night in Creede*

## CURLY BILL AND SKELETON CANYON

"How heavy were the gold bars Curly Bill's gang stole anyway?" Uncle Wayne asked.

"Well," I said, "from what I've read the bricks were probably two to three hundred pounds each. Made it impossible for pack mules to carry them off in case of a stage robbery."

"Yeah," Mike said, "it would take two bricks to make a pack balance, way too heavy for any pack animal besides a camel or elephant!"

Uncle Wayne chuckled and said, "Besides that a camel or elephant would be easy trackin'. Each dung pile'd fill an ore car."

"My theory is," I said, "the robbers chopped the bars in half with axes. I cut a ten pound lead weight with my hatchet, you know, off the old weight belt from our underwater dredging days, to test my theory."

"You what?" Mike said.

I ignored Mike's reprimand and went on. "Easier than cutting some of the meat we dried. And pure gold is soft like lead. A big stout horse or mule could pack three hundred pounds fast, for awhile anyway."

"But," Mike said, "they sure couldn't outrun a posse. That's why when their pack horses gave out somewhere around here, they stopped." He paused, put a match to his cigar, and took satisfying drag. "I read that Dutch John was a mean old fart, and treated the fifteen year like a slave and threatened to kill the boy, take the one good horse and hide all the gold. So when Dutch passed out, Little Dave cut off his head with an axe. Little Dave buried the gold bar halves, and probably shaved off some gold and left for Oklahoma Territory. He didn't want to be hung for robbery and murder. Then supposedly two years later he returned to dig up the gold, but everything looked different. The old trail and campsite washed away and Granite Gap a booming mining camp."

Mike poked the fire and put the last mesquite sticks in, the small fire crackled, the smoke and boiling coffee smelled good. The only trees left were shrub size twisted juniper and mesquite.

Miners cut any decent trees over a century ago, and later cowboys used wood for fence posts and branding fires. Oh well, I thought, plenty of sticks, cactus skeletons, and cowpies for a campfire.

Mike reached over to toss a dried cow flop in the fire.

"Dammit Mike," I said, "at least wait, I do draw the line at cooking hotdogs in smoking cow turds."

Uncle Wayne laughed and slapped his knee, "You sure are getting picky in your old age Jill."

I reached down and threw a large cowpie at him, he ducked. I said, "You're lucky we aren't tracking elephants and camels!"

After dinner of hot dogs, beans, and coffee, the three of us sat back smoking cigars. We breathed in the aroma of our Cuban seed cigars from Mexico and the New Mexican roasted cow flops. Actually I thought to myself, both smells are quite similar.

Uncle Wayne said, "All these old lost treasure legends are fun to think about, but where are the hard cold facts, evidence? I think they're just a bunch of stories made up to sell more treasure hunting paraphernalia!" I saw Mike sit up straight and square his shoulders to respond. Uncle Wayne will get what he wanted. A good heated argument. I can still remember a remark Uncle Wayne made years ago when our canoe capsized on the South Fork of the Forty Mile River in Alaska, "It's accidents and arguments that make life interesting."

A few crickets trilled, the small fire popped and hissed, and the donkeys munched dried grass. In a month thousands of chirping crickets would dominate the warm evening air. Nights now were too cool for rattlers, scorpions, and fire ants. Was a peaceful in-between time in the desert. We relaxed unmolested by dive bombing, biting, and stinging bugs.

The donkeys even ignored the smoky fire. During insect season, the donkeys crowd close to the campfire smoke. Once Shaggy backed too near the fire and singed his tail. Donkeys are not afraid of smoke and fire.

The pile of treasures we found using our metal detectors shown in the firelight—some old conchos, a rusted cavalry canteen, lots of well worn horse, mule and donkey shoes, tobacco cans, a rusty rifle barrel, and some promising looking ore that probably fell off a mule drawn ore wagon. No gold bricks, no Spanish silver.

Mike took a deep breath, turned toward Uncle Wayne and said, "Me and Jill didn't believe all those miners, prospectors, and thieves could possibly lose or stash sacks of gold, or find rich veins of ore and never find them again. Of course unless they died or something. But we went prospecting in Southeast Utah canyon country and got lost. Our compasses acted funny and the wind blew covering most our tracks. A few piles of donkey dung and Jill's rock cairns got us back to base camp the next day."

Mike paused, took a sip of coffee, puffed on his cigar and continued. "That was before we bought the Global Positioning unit. People can get dazed and disoriented from exhaustion, thirst, hunger, and fear, then wander around for days...and remember, Jill, in Idaho you lost a vial of gold when you cleaned the sluice, the mosquitoes so thick you used your jacket with the gold vial in the pocket to swat at them? Then later in the season I lost a vial full of mercury, gold, and silver out of my shirt pocket while crawling around looking for a tiny nut and bolt.

Both times we finally made the journey back to base camp, got the metal detector and found the lost vials, and nut and bolt." Mike took another puff on his cigar. "My point is, Wayne, that in frontier times no one had metal detectors, easy to read compasses, topo maps, aerial photos, GPS units, and RV's parked two miles away loaded with water and provisions . . . So I think a person could lose gold and search his entire life in the wrong canyon for that gold vein or buried treasure he stashed or found once, and walk days in a big circle and die with the mystery unsolved. With metal detectors, maps, perseverance and luck we have lots better odds finding all sorts of lost or buried stuff."

"But," Wayne asked, "if any of this buried treasure is found, who is gunna know? If it's worth millions like the buried loot Skeleton Canyon claims, would you personally tell the world and get it stolen by a museum or the feds? HELL NO YOU WOULDN'T, so you don't even know if these gold bars are still here!"

"Wait a minute," Mike interrupted, "I've got that all figured out. We only know a fraction of what really was buried, stolen, and lost. Most folks would be too proud and embarrassed to brag about their dumbness. So usually while we're lookin for one thing we find something else."

Uncle Wayne leaned back, puffed on his cigar, sipped cold coffee, thinking. Then he said, "I'll get out my treasure dousing rods tomorrow. I just happened to bring them along." I stifled a laugh.

Mike stared at him disbelieving. "I thought you only cared about placer gold. I thought you were only humoring us looking for treasure?"

Uncle Wayne said "And maybe next week we can haul the donkeys and our gear down to Skeleton Canyon and do a little exploring. I was reading that Skeleton Canyon is on a smugglers' trail and had a steady stream of contraband, from cattle to pesos, that flowed back and forth from Old Mexico to Tombstone and Tucson. The canyon, perfect for ambushing unsuspecting pack trains.

"I also read in 1881 a large Mexican pack train carrying a gold shipment was attacked in Skeleton Canyon. From human bones recovered they think about nineteen men were killed and none of the gold showed up in the area. Curly Bill Brocius was mentioned as one of the gang leaders involved. Same fella that masterminded the 1882 Benson-Tombstone stage robbery, the eight bandits split up and two of them stopped here at Granite Gap, Dutch John and Little Dave."

Uncle Wayne and I sat near the dying fire, smiling. Mike looked puzzled. "Darn you Wayne, I thought you were a treasure huntin skeptic."

"Nope," Uncle Wayne said, "just wanted to get some lively conversation going. It's accidents and arguments that make life interesting. Well I'm going to hit the sack, lots of washes and old camps we haven't hunted in yet."

"Goodnight Uncle Wayne, you rascal," I said as I crawled into my sleeping bag. Klondike Mike stirred the dying coals of the cow flop fire, a smile on his face.

## HOT HIGH NOON
## Outlaw Trail, Granite Gap

Nauseated and dizzy I trudged forward, sweat burned my eyes. The donkeys plodded, heads down, eyes half closed. "C'mon Willy and Shag, we've got to reach the mine tunnel, it'll be cool, we can rest."

Another earth cracking, sky bleaching, Southwest summer day. The moment the sun appeared it blazed hot. Shade temperatures reached 108 to 110 by noon. All wise desert creatures hid this time of day, except buzzards, who soared high above the searing heat. Prickly pear, low chaparral, and sagebrush scattered in the red streaked rocks offered no escape for large mammals.

This moisture sucking furnace made me ache for another Alaska summer. I'd trade working in ice cold water, putting up with mosquitoes and no-see-ums any day for the battalions of drumming, lantern smashing moths, the Tartar hordes of marching red ants, nearly foot long centipedes, and the scurrying secretive straw colored scorpions that invade the stifling hot nights. But at least we have the cool depths of the mine tunnels for retreat.

Each donkey carried two three-gallon water cans, plus grain, some canned food (handy in the desert because they contain water), pick, hammer, ore sacks, flashlights, candles, matches, hard hat. Two days before we hauled up my camping gear, cot, more water, and provisions. We'd stay till our water and grain ran out then haul ore down the mountain, pick up more water, grain, and supplies and hike back to the mine.

We turned off Cowboy Pass Trail and headed east up Outlaw Trail. "C'mon boys, we can do it. Only a half mile more." Willy and Shag perked up. They knew this route led to rest and cold air from a well ventilated roomy mine tunnel.

I stopped the donkeys twice, each time to drink another quart of water. My face burned red hot despite the wide brimmed straw hat I wore. Even the donkeys were sweating, and a donkey doesn't sweat easily. I stumbled toward the tunnel entrance, blinded by the burning sweat. The cold air hit my sun baked body. "Ah, thank

God!" I said, "we're finally here!" But Shag jerked on the lead rope and pulled me backwards, then I heard the angry buzz of a rattlesnake a few paces in front of me.

"Damn," in my bumbling I almost stepped on the three foot diamondback, or was it a Mojave? I picked up a boulder and with both hands lobbed it onto the rattler's head. He thrashed and flung around for awhile. His head was crushed but he was still dangerous, so I rammed my boot onto his skull and cut his head off with my knife. I speared the fanged head with the long knife, examined it and put it under a big boulder away from the mine tunnel. "Well, boys," I said, "got fresh meat for my evening meal. Not quite like catching grayling from the South Fork of the Fortymile, but it'll do."

*Crotalus scutulatus.* Mojave rattlesnake. This species base color is often green, this one was salmon colored, but had the Mojave identifiers: Two or three small scales between the supraoculars (the large scales above the eyes), the western diamondback has four or more smaller scales between the supraoculars. The second identifier is the black-and-white tail bands called a "coon-tail." The diamondback's bands are nearly equal in width, the Mojave's white bands are wider than the black bands. The most important difference is the venom toxicity. The Mojave venom has been compared to the neurotoxins in the bite of the deadly Taipan and coral snake.

Dreamily I said, "Maybe next summer though we might head up the Al-Can Highway, heard it's mostly paved now, look at some Yukon placers. Maybe even see who is still dredging on the South

Fork of the Forty Mile River and then mosey on over near Trapper Creek and Cache Creek."

I sighed and continued unloading the donkeys in the cavern like room near the mine tunnel entrance. I gave Shag and Willy some grain and a bucket of water, and kept talking to my long eared companions.

"After a siesta I'll skin and gut the snake. I know blood and guts don't bother you donkeys. Remember when you guys packed out a bear and later a cougar for those two hunters? You both plodded along poker faced, no fuss. The hunters used a horse the year before. It bucked and kicked, broke one hunter's kneecap, then the horse crashed through some fir trees, ripped the bear hide to shreds and bruised the heck out of the meat! That will teach them to use a dumb horse, isn't that right boys?" The donkeys ignored me and continued munching on their grain and sucked water from the bucket.

This little room off the tunnel entrance was once an outlaw hideout according to local legend. Though only two horses with riders, bedrolls, and a small campfire would fit, most the notorious gangs rode in groups of eight to twenty riders, although they sometimes dispersed in twos after a robbery—with my metal detector I did find some conchos and two spurs, so I guess it could be an old hideout. Shag, Willy, me and my cot and small fire fit perfectly.

From the cool safety of the mine portal I looked east to the Pyramid Mountains. Animas Valley shimmered in the heat waves, the sky white hot.

Uncle Wayne went north to his ranch and placer mine in the Okanogan. Mike was at Red Rock looking for rock houses and cliff dwellings.

Before Uncle Wayne left he said, "I'm going to work down here in the winter and go north in the summer. Next summer might even head to Nome, Alaska. Never been there, heard there's good ground, lots of placer gold, and great fishing. Well, I'll see you all in October when it cools down . . . don't fry your brains, ha! ha!"

I leaned back against the cool rock wall, closed my eyes and dreamed of moose, caribou, bears and wild blueberries, huge mountain beaver slapped their tails on ponds, grayling and salmon jumped in the rivers, and gold glowed in my sluice box.

## SEARCHING TO FIND EL DORADO
### Coronado National Forest

The wind picked up blowing in our faces. A persistent tune from an old western movie filled my brain and I sang:

... *Through sunshine and shadow, from darkness till noon; Over mountains that reach from the sky to the moon; A man with a dream that will never let go; Keep searching to find El Dorado; So ride boldly ride to the end of the rainbow; Ride boldly ride till you find El Dorado* ...

The wind roared through the piñon pine and junipers. Mike interrupted my solo and yelled, "THE WIND'S GETTING WORSE, WE BETTER FIND SHELTER!"

I checked my compass and shot a reading south 35 degrees west, and shouted back, "SHOULD BE MINES AND DUMPS AHEAD, MAYBE A TUNNEL!"

We stumbled on, heads bent, the gritty sand blinded us. I held tight to Willy's lead rope. "C'mon boy, help me, I can't see. Keep us on the trail."

... *Thou winds become bitter the sky turns to grey; His body grows weary, he can't find his way; But he'll never turn back, though he's lost in the snow; For he has to find El Dorado* ...

According to my research this obscure and hopefully abandoned part of a smugglers trail passed through remote roadless mining camps in the Coronado National Forest.

Willy stopped near a pile of old timbers, once a head frame over a mine shaft. "Now hopefully," I said to myself, "We'll find a cozy tunnel."

We scrambled around the heap of wood and I heard Mike shout, "OVER HERE, A TUNNEL!"

"Thank God."

At the tunnel entrance the donkeys perked up. Shaggy pushed ahead trying to enter the tunnel first, but the bulging panniers stopped him. Mike coaxed Shaggy back and removed his top pack and panniers. I unloaded Willy and dropped the boxes, tarps, lash cinch and line at the tunnel entrance. We found our flashlights and hard hats. The donkeys restless and anxious to get out of the storm. We trusted Willy's and Shaggy's judgement, so all four of us in single file entered the rock sanctuary.

Mike went first holding Shag's lead. I unsnapped Willy's lead rope, and let him follow Shaggy and Mike. I dragged the pannier boxes and top packs behind us, and stacked the gear along the tunnel ribs.

A light breeze blew at our backs. Sign of good ventilation, and an easy way to find our way out. If the breeze is at our backs going in it will be in our faces going out. I made arrows on the floor with rocks, just in case.

After walking about a hundred-fifty feet we came to three drifts. We turned left and followed the drift with the best air. The donkeys walked quietly, alert. They crouched and slid under low spots in the tunnel.

We noticed a set of boot-prints and other smaller tennis shoe prints. Most tunnels are explored periodically by hunters and mineral collectors. Tracks difficult to date this far underground; no rain, no earth moving winds, few animals ventured far in total blackness, except bats. Undisturbed footprints can last indefinitely.

The tunnel back and ribs expanded. White quartz stringers lined the rock walls. Our lights reflected off the quartz and brightened our way.

We entered an open stope cavern. On a rock face around a bend we saw a yellow light flickering.

Mike said, "What the?"

"SHH!" I snapped. Then we heard a muffled clatter and scraping. The donkeys looked curious, but not alarmed. I whispered, "Let's go see."

"No," Mike said, "you stay here."

"No way, I'm going too." Mike tied Shaggy to a piece of ore car track. We moved ahead, hesitant, our flashlights facing downward. I clutched my light, my heart pounded.

A small fire twinkled ahead. Gallon plastic water jugs littered the floor. A coffee can with a baling wire handle lay near the fire, its contents spilled.

"Hello?" I said, "Anybody here?" Then I heard a child cry. A man stepped from the shadows holding a large rock then a teenage boy emerged holding a stick of wood.

I put my flashlight down and raised my hands slowly, palms out, to show no weapons. We left our pistols in coat pockets at the tunnel entrance in the panniers. Dumb.

Mike showed his empty hands and moved toward the dying fire, righted the ruined pot of beans, and said, "Sorry."

A young woman dressed in men's clothes, holding a toddler, stepped out. The little boy looked at us with big dark eyes, his cheeks tear stained.

I pointed to the bean can and pointed back where we came. "I'll get more food."

Something moved up behind us. I could feel the warm breath. My knees buckled and I almost fainted. The Mexicans gasped. Willy stuck his grey head and huge ears between Mike and I, then proceeded to walk forward and nibble at the spilled beans. Everyone laughed and the woman exclaimed, "Burro! Si, burro! Gracias." Everyone relaxed.

I said to Mike, "I hope they don't want to eat him."

Through gestures and sign language I explained we had food and water to share. We walked Willy and Shaggy to the panniers and loaded the canned chili, ham, sardines, crackers, raisins, energy bars, coffee and pot, and other stuff, put it all in garbage bags and dangled them from the packsaddles. Mike and I carried the three gallon water containers to the underground hideout.

This time we packed our guns. Here near the Mexico border, historically a major smuggling route for cattle, horses, pesos, gold, silver, and slaves; now used for smuggling drugs and young illegal farm workers. Are these people drug "mules" paid by border "coyotes" or a poor family fleeing poverty in search of work?

We walked back to the campfire. My feet and hands sweating, my mouth dry with fear. Were ten more people hiding? Waiting to kill us? Would there be an underground shootout?

The donkeys remained passive. We unloaded everything. And Mike gestured about firewood. The man replied, "Si, Si." and pointed to a side drift. Mike moved his light and saw a collapsed wood ore chute. The men and boy carried pieces of rough cut lumber to the campfire.

Over a dinner of chili, canned ham, raisins and hot coffee they told us their names which I could not pronounce. Seems they were meeting a relative near Tucson and would work on a ranch. The fire burned out while we slept. The donkeys woke us about 7 a.m., their normal breakfast time. In the blackness and silence of a mine tunnel time of day seemed irrelevant.

We left all our food with the Mexican family. Filled all the their water jugs, gave them two canteens, two ore sacks, matches, flashlight batteries, candles, some garbage bags, a wool blanket, a hand drawn map, and two rolls of TP. On the map I marked creeks and springs I thought had water, and stock tanks plus routes to highways. If they got into trouble the Border Patrol could pick them up, give them medical attention. We bid the family "Adios, and good luck."

Outside we fed and watered the donkeys, balanced their packs and loaded the panniers and top packs, threw some diamond hitches over the works. Two gallons of water left, no food, time to head back to the truck and stock trailer. The metal detectors wrapped and unused in the panniers. We walked down the mountain in silence. The canyon wrens sang, the sky cold blue.

*. . . Over mountains that reach from the sky to the moon; A man with a dream that will never let go; Keep searching to find El Dorado; So ride boldly ride to the end of the rainbow; Ride boldly ride till you find El Dorado . . .*
Tears dripped down the front of my jacket.

## DON QUOXITE AND SANCHO PANZA
### Summer, Mogollon Mountains, New Mexico

There are strange things done in the midnight sun
By the men who moil for gold...
*— Robert W. Service*

Klondike Mike and I sat around the fragrant piñon pine and juniper campfire. The canyon walls glowed hot orange. A still night except for the low gurgle of the creek and the chirping crickets.

"Mike, we've been here at Lost Creek Canyon almost five weeks, panning, sluicing, digging and hammering rocks. Got some gold but the creek is slowing down, and all we've seen is one geologist, one forest ranger, five deer, one badger and one coyote. I want to do something different, something exciting . . . while we're waiting for the summer rains. You know, a break from all this serious work."

"Oh, no!" Klondike Mike groaned. "Now what do you want to do? Isn't this an adventure? So far we got charged by a cow moose in Idaho, and then remember outside Death Valley a feral jack trotted into camp, kicking and biting, trying to steal our jennets? Then in Colorado the rangy looking black bear that circled and lurked around camp for two days, and our shovels and stuff got buried and we found—"

"But that was months ago!" I interrupted. Mike shot me a dirty look. "I know. OK, OK. You're right but—"

"But what Jill?" Do you have to get scared out of your wits to be content?"

"No I don't! You're just jumping to conclusions. I had something different in mind."

Mike leaned back and sighed, "Oh God, what is it this time?"

"Well, let's pretend you're Don Quoxite, and Shaggy can be 'Rosinante,' Don Quoxite's faithful steed, and I'll be Sancho Panza. Willy can be 'Dapple,' Sancho's trusty steed."

Then in my theatrical voice I said, "TOMORROW WE SHALL DEPART ON A QUEST!"

"A quest for what?" Mike asked.

"WE SHALL BE ON A QUEST FOR ADVENTURE, my dear Don Quoxite."

Klondike Mike being a good sport replied in his canyon theater voice, "HARK! I HEARETH THE LION DRAGON ROAR IN YONDER HILLS—I SHALL GATHER MY LANCE AND YOU YOUR BOW AND ARROWS, AND WE SHALL SLAY THE EVIL BEAST!" Then added, "Tomorrow after breakfast."

I guffawed with laughter and fell off my little fold up canvas stool.

The next morning we saddled and packed "Rosinante" and "Dapple." Then added makeshift costumes to ourselves and our two faithful steeds. Don Quoxite mounted Rosinante and I, Sancho Panza, mounted Dapple, and we rode out of the canyon to yonder hills.

Our faithful steeds wore helmets made with silver duct tape and my faded pink cotton underwear. Their large ears stuck out the leg holes. Our jackets became coats of armor when worn backwards. We taped our green plastic gold pans upside down on our cowboy hats as our helmets. A colorful blanket laid out full over each steed's saddle, rump and neck; armor to deflect the blows and hot fiery breath of our enemies.

Don Quoxite shouted, "BEWARE SANCHO A GIANT CARNIVORE BUFFALO STANDS AHEAD READY TO KILL AND DEVOUR US, MAKE HASTE WITH BOW AND

ARROWS AND I WITH MY LANCE! CHARGE SANCHO! CHARGE!"

We trotted (because the donkeys wouldn't gallop) toward the massive boulder shaped like a buffalo. Don Quoxite had his lance (actually a wimpy stick) and I Sancho, my bow and arrows (a thin sapling bent with the elastic band from Willy's pink helmet for the bow string and twigs for arrows). The bow propelled the arrows about two and a half feet.

"DEATH TO YOU OH MURDEROUS BEAST! YOU HAVE KILLED YOUR LAST TRAVELER! TAKE THAT! AND THAT!" shouted Don Quoxite brandishing his lance.

After a day and a half of battles we decided to head back to the castle.

We reached a forest service road still in costume. We followed this road about two miles and were ready to turn south off the gravel into Lost Creek Canyon, when around the bend a Winnebago appeared. Our laughing, singing and loud monologues drowned out the engine noise. Oops, too late to hide.

"Oh damn! Mike what should we do?"

"SANCHO, IS THIS THE LION DRAGON WE'VE BEEN HUNTING? BRANDISH YOUR WEAPONS. PREPARE TO ATTACK!"

"No Mike! Come on, act normal!"

The Winnebago crept by. I waved with my bow and Mike tipped his green duct taped helmet. The donkeys curious, watched the coach pass. Their huge ears stuck out of duct taped pink underwear. The two couples in the motorhome stared at us with blank expressions, no one waved or smiled.

After they passed we burst into gut wrenching laughter. I slid off Willy and rolled on the roadside clutching my sides, gasping for air.

Mike said between strangled gulps, "We better get off this road before a forest ranger or somebody else shows up."

One look at Mike and Shaggy and I started laughing all over again and couldn't get back in the saddle. I ran, clutching myself, into the woods before I peed my pants.

Willy, Mike and Shaggy left me rolling around on the ground. Eventually I gained enough composure to walk the mile or so back to camp.

Mike had a small fire going. We unloaded the donkeys and removed their costumes. I threw the wads of duct tape into the fire, and saved the undies for rags.

We watched Shaggy and Willy roll while we sat at the pine slab table that Mike built.

"Now that was a great adventure!" I said.

"Amen," said Mike, "And here's to the silver tape knights of the pine slab table!" We lifted our tin cups of powdered milk and drank.

## QUEST

"No, you can't come with us. We are on a quest," I replied. Roger asked again if he could go prospecting with Mike, me, and the donkeys.

Roger was a truck driver, stuck for a week, waiting for his empty trailer from Mexico.

I sighed and thought to myself; we've done this before; another body to feed, being jabbered at when I don't feel like jabbering. Some guests try to be helpful . . . Doreen and Ron from New York cooked three days of food rations for dinner one evening, then the next morning they had the donkeys saddled, packed and ready to go. The packsaddles were on backwards.

I prefer privacy so I can stare at rocks and terrain features without pretending to know anything. The other problem, personal hygiene. I'd have to bathe under my army poncho and walk a mile away to squat. And I couldn't put my rinsed undies up close to the fire next to the bean pot.

Roger interrupted my musing and said, "I'll pay you?"

I cleared my throat and Klondike Mike coughed. "Well," I said "that changes everything. How much?" Mike and Roger agreed on one-hundred fifty dollars for three days, if he helped with the camp chores.

"And," I said, "we aren't turning back if you get bored, and all we have to eat is beans, biscuits, some dried stuff, and army rations. No cream, no sugar, no mayo, and what we call prospectors' coffee looks and tastes like black mud."

"That sounds great!" Roger replied cheerfully.

Klondike Mike grinned and said, "Cash up front, no refunds, and you have to sign this liability release."

"No problem. Makes it seem," Roger replied, " more risky and exciting."

"Nope," I said, "you'll more likely die of boredom."

Some folks imagine treasure hunting and prospecting expeditions should resemble a *Raiders of the Lost Ark* adventure. But prospecting and camping in remote areas is mainly a lot of routine chores: mostly firewood gathering, hauling water, filtering water, boiling water, sifting through dirt, cooking, dealing with thunderstorms, rodents, and repair of damaged gear—made more difficult and

lengthy due to lack of modern conveniences, like hot running water out of a faucet, a refrigerator, electricity . . .

"Did anyone bring the lantern mantles?" "Damn! The vacuum packed, strawberry jam leaked and squished all over the clean socks. Hope the fire ants aren't out yet."

The second day prospecting with Roger, the donkeys wandered off and we spent most the day searching. Then we found them two hundred feet away behind large granite boulders under a cottonwood tree swishing their tails.

Occasionally and usually at 3 a.m., one of the donkeys gives a sort of cough-snort warning (the same sound an angry moose makes) when something is lurking around; mostly we never see the lurker, but suffer mainly from lack of sleep.

Some days are spent in utter laziness which often makes visitors uncomfortable and restless.

The last evening camping with Roger when the sun went down, a few stray clouds caught fire. What sounded like a mountain lion scream echoed in the canyon. The mesquite fire danced magic under the desert sky and gleamed off wind polished agates like tigers' eyes. The limestone cliffs glowed with veins of rose quartz; like writing on the wall, "GOD WAS HERE."

## KELLY MINE OR BUST
### Magdalena, New Mexico

The offer to live at the Kelly Mine during the summer tourist season came via snail mail (as opposed to e-mail, which we didn't have).

We boarded up the mine shack at Granite Gap, loaded the donkeys, and headed north. Blue tarps flapped in our rear view mirrors; my mottled brown Ford truck pulled an elderly stock trailer and Mike's dented vari-colored GMC towed a 70's vintage travel trailer; the Squattley's on the move . . . again. Kelly Mine Or Bust.

Kelly, a ghost town and mine is located in the Magdalena Mountains of New Mexico, seven thousand feet elevation. Three thousand people once lived at the old town-site. Full scale mining started in 1879 and ended about 1945.

The Bureau of Mines reported Kelly important as a lead silver, zinc, and copper producing mine. Gold not listed as significant.

One retired miner laughed, slapped his thigh and said "Ha! There was so much gold and high-gradin' going on . . . wasn't reported, wasn't on the books . . . gol dang I got medicine bottles full of gold me and my pop high-graded outa here. I'll show ya! We was rich! The mine supers was rich!"

He paused to spit a brown stream of tobacco and continued still grinning. "They sold the gold, you know, the black market—got lots more than the feds 'ed give em. Ha! You better believe it!" He paused and spat again. "You don't report stuff unless your gunna sell, then you salt the hell out the mine—if you got thousands of ounces comin' out of the ground, why sell? An, if it ain't worth a damn you sell and lie like all hell fire. Just ask anybody that mined here, they'll tell ya. There's a few of us still kickin."

We did ask around. The miners, or their sons, and grandsons, told similar stories.

"Yep," another old timer remarked, "had me a claim near the top of that ridge." He pointed his gnarled bony finger toward a ridge and saddle about a mile southwest. "And had me two mules, one for ridin' and one for packin'. Rough goin'. Game trails, no roads. Gold got real important after the government dropped the silver standard in 1893; that's what my uncle told me. He's dead now. He said there was gold up high. He was right. And something else . . . " He pointed to the location of one of the tunnels at Kelly. "The small amount of gold that was reported mined here—see that dump half way down the mountain? Says it came from there, but the actual deposit was up yonder," he pointed again, this time northeast, "on the other side of that hill."

Every miner or his living kin in this town has native gold in nuggets and in quartz (which isn't supposed to be found here), and every miner or his kin has museum and the gem grade zinc ore called smithsonite, also found here.

High-grading like salting was so prevalent and rarely mentioned in mine engineer textbooks, but could make or break a mining operation. From the miners' point of view, pocketing small amounts of rich ore was a traditional part of the job. Many superintendents turned a blind eye toward high-grading among the miners, not wanting to antagonize them into slowdown reprisals, and also justifying low wages.

Smithsonite is now selling by the carat. "Dang, we used chunks of it for doorstops," one of the villagers remarked. Most windowsills in the village of Magdalena (three miles north of Kelly) hold large dusty fist size pieces of azurite and smithsonite setting beside purple glass bottles.

When the mine closed, residents of Kelly dismantled their homes and rebuilt in Magdalena where electricity and indoor plumbing was available.

The Kelly mine dumps and ghost town held gold, and the famous translucent blue-green smithsonite, azurite, bottles, coins, a treasure hunters paradise.

Willy and Shaggy fidgeted, anxious to explore new ground. Mike packed Shaggy and I saddled and loaded Willy.

Mike said, "Let's head up high where the gold is."

I replied, "Of course."

Shaggy shook his head up and down, and brayed, as if to say, "C'mon hurry up, I'm tired of standing here."

## MULE AND DONKEY RIDE AND DRIVE

### Reprinted from *Magdalena Mountain Mail* April, 1999

The Rio Grande Mule and Donkey Association is sponsoring a ride and drive at the Magdalena Rodeo and Fairgrounds April 24th and 25th. You may arrive on Friday evening April 23rd, camping and corrals available.

Don Thornton said, "These are fun days, no clinics, no seminars. Just about any critter is welcome, including zebras, zonkeys (zebra/donkey cross), zorses (zebra/horse cross); although we do hesitate with emus and ostriches, as they upset and offend the equines.

The wagons and riders will leave the fairgrounds toward Riley about 10 a.m. Saturday and stop at Bear Springs turn off for lunch, and hopefully find a few shade trees. Then return to the fairgrounds about 4 p.m.

Anyone curious or interested in seeing what donkeys and mules can do, or just plain bored with cruising up and down Main Street is welcome. Saturday evening we will have a campfire (if winds permit) and a potluck dinner. Everyone (except emus and ostriches) is invited to join us.


## HIGH WINDS DIDN'T STOP THESE ASSES

Saturday morning Apr. 24 trailers with horses, mules and donkeys pulled into the Magdalena Rodeo grounds. The wind blew sand in our faces. But we didn't care. Sixteen riders: men, women, kids. I heard someone yell, "Let's get our asses down the road!"

The motley procession began... Marcia Thornton's jack (this is a fully intact stud donkey) named Jack took the bit in his teeth (which means the rider loses control, also known as a runaway) and charged after Willy.

Willy a gelded donkey loaded with box panniers containing, lunch, cameras, water, and other stuff; was attacked from behind by Jack. Willy's lead was tied to my donkey's saddle. The pursuit was on. Two riders, three donkeys raced around the fairgrounds. Marcia jumped off as Jack came down on top of Willy. With help from cowboys, Curley and Tony, Marcia untangled the pack gear and donkeys.

Marcia returned to the corrals to teach Jack trail manners

Meanwhile... on the road to Riley, Jane Jasper and her daughter, Aspen (from Los Lunas) rode Jane's famous mammoth white ass Levi. Earl Coble from Belen rode his mule Festus; Diane Nicholson, from Belen, on her stripe legged mule Matilda. Seventeen year old Miss Hartley from Socorro rode her State Fair winner, Apache, a hinny. Camilla Maluotoga and Henry Ford, of Los Lunas, brought Madeline an adopted feral burro trained for competition, and a gaited mammoth donkey named Pacha.

Rio Grande Mule and Donkey Association President, Robert Auge, and Nelda Auge from Belen brought Packy a donkey and Saffron a horse.

The "Magdalena Bunch" – "Curley" Bowden on his horse R.C.; Tony Trujillo on Mosca a horse. Don Thornton was riding a horse he called Molasses. I rode Raymond, a donkey. And our newest and youngest member Daniel Otero rode Shaggy.

The following day most the above folks were ready again to ride and drive. Tony and Don brought the buckboard wagon. Marcia and Camilla drove a two wheel buggy pulled by Madeline, and Packy pulled Nelda in their cart.

A busted latigo left me in a ditch straddling an empty saddle, but thanks to my packer's repair kit (baling twine and duct tape) our pack string eventually caught up; although I missed the wagon gully jump, and another runaway chase.

During dinner, talk was of trail tales and plans for donkey and mule games: obstacle courses, barrel racing, packing races and preparing for the New Mexico State Fair Mule and Donkey Show. A date was set for another Rio Grande Mule and Donkey Association action packed outing.

## SMILIN' JACK AND THE LOST GOLD MINE
### Magdalena Mountains

From Chihuahua Gulch we rode toward Pony Spring and the abandoned mines below Little Baldy Mountain. We turned east on a game trail and meandered into a steep narrow cadmium orange canyon. This time of year the spring water barely trickled and left only small puddles.

Swarms of flies droned. A small flock of Gambel's quail with their teardrop-shaped head plumes dashed and cackled ahead of us. Canyon wrens sang descending series of clear whistled notes. Mourning doves cooed and piñon jays laughed and chattered. Rock squirrels squeaked, scurried about, and peeked at us from their shelters.

I sat relaxed in the old McClellan cavalry saddle, and imagined life here 100 years ago.

We followed a treasure map crudely drawn by Smilin' Jack, a 97 year old toothless man, whose uncle (long since dead) once had a gold claim up here—somewhere.

Smilin' Jack remembered Alka Seltzer bottles full of gold buttons, and vaguely remembered the location of his uncle's mine. He wanted us to find it before he died.

We wrote up a 50/50 agreement. Fifty percent to him and his heirs, fifty percent to us.

Mike was riding Shaggy a hundred feet behind Willy and I. Willy had a quick, impatient gait; Shaggy plodded, sniffed, inspected, contemplated. I wanted Willy to slow down and Mike wanted Shaggy to hurry up. Sometimes we'd switch mounts. Shag and I would plod, sniff, inspect, contemplate, and rest often; lagging sometimes a quarter mile behind. This irritated Klondike Mike and Willy.

After turning into a juniper and scrub oak canyon I noticed a subtle change; the birds no longer sang; it seemed quiet, too quiet. I thought, *good place for an ambush* ...

Willy stopped abruptly, snorted, wheeled around, and trotted back a few steps. Shaggy jumped into the air and turned 360 degrees. Both donkeys stared, huge ears pointed into a thick clump of junipers. I attempted to spring from my saddle (like they do in the movies) but my left hiking boot (improper footwear for riding) got stuck in the stirrup. I flopped under Willy, and managed to pull my sweaty stocking foot out of my trapped boot, and rolled out of Willy's way. Next to my face was a steaming blob full of juniper berries, insect carapaces, and unidentifiable fibrous clumps.

In riding style, I resembled Humpty Dumpty, but Mike was still astride Shaggy–his long grasshopper legs dangled near the ground, his saddle and gear only slightly disheveled.

The donkeys stared, ears forward. Shaggy coughed a warning. Willy snorted, stomped, pawed the ground, and strutted toward the junipers. Mike and I drew our pistols simultaneously; I, a two inch barrel .38, useless past five feet; Mike, a long barrel .22 pistol loaded with birdshot for killing rattlesnakes, also useless.

The tree rustled, branches moved; two bright beady eyes peered out. Willy charged forward. I fired one warning shot into a stump. Branches swooshed. We heard a muffled grunt, and soft padding sounds retreated; then silence. A cinnamon phase sow and her black cub moved like phantoms along an invisible trail on the canyon wall. Willy shook his head, pawed the ground, and let out an echoing bray. We all watched the bears glide away.

The bear blob glistened, birds flitted by and sang again.

We continued past scrub oak, piñon pine, juniper trees, cane cholla and prickly pear. I walked leading Willy behind Shag and Mike. Only a mile to go before we'd set up camp and start hunting in earnest.

Smilin' Jack's lost mine could be buried under a landslide; could be owned by a Canadian mining company; could be . . . We didn't care. Still, better odds than buying a lottery ticket.

Up ahead Mike yelled, "Jill, get up here! Look at this!"

I mumbled to myself, "This better be worth the hurry."

"Jill, look at this! An azurite outcropping."

I held a sky blue rock in my hand and tapped it with a hammer. This exposed a cluster of deep blue azurite crystals.

"Nice stuff," I admitted. "Looks like gem grade, after you get rid of the oxidized stuff." I recited, "Copper carbonate. An important copper ore. Some of the big mining operations crush this stuff up."

Mike got out his GPS Unit to record our location. He said, "Maybe we can file a claim, work here while we search for Smilin' Jack's gold mine."

"Sounds good to me. There's pyrites here too. Old timers said gold was found here with sulfides, like pyrite."

We untied our jumbled bedrolls and supplies from the donkeys' saddles. Jerky, coffee, dried fruit, canteens, tin can for making coffee, hammers, and flashlights were all stuffed in ore sacks. Didn't bring much for one night; only had two days off from tourists at the Kelly Mine.

While I tethered the donkeys, I told them, "Enough grama grass and water seeping in this puddle for you two. Hope it rains soon, don't want to haul water up here next week when we search for Smilin' Jack's lost gold mine." The donkeys ignored me. Shaggy sucked water from the spring seep and Willy chewed on dry grass.

## CAMP CUISINE

### September, Cibola National Forest, New Mexico

The high desert monsoon season was over. The pale green tough grama grass would bleach and die. Desert downpours had flushed the landscape, washed away roads, and carved out new ravines; the dry earth, like a sponge, sucked the water away. The mineral and treasure rich land gouged open. El Dorado.

The pack gear was laid out around me, I sat on a canvas camp stool sorting and arranging the piles of what looked like junk for my next pack trip in search of Smilin' Jack's lost gold mine.

Smilin' Jack's old miner friend Bill, showed me some samples of azurite webbed with golden threads. Said he found those rare specimens on the same mountain.

In a plastic bag I had Smilin' Jack's lost gold mine map; a hardback copy of *Horses, Hitches & Rocky Trails* "The Packers Bible" by Joe Back; *A Field Guide To Animal Tracks*; National Audubon Society *Field Guide To North American Rocks And Minerals*; *Western Mining* by Otis Young; and A Sierra Club Totebook, *Cooking For Camp And Trail*.

I hadn't read the pocket cookbook yet so I thumbed through it. The donkeys were standing around bored, trying to steal my already donkey chewed straw hat.

The cute orange colored waterproof book's introduction said it was written for people who don't want to face another can of Vienna sausage and fried Spam luncheon meat . . . for those traveling "by car, raft, row boat, pack animal and dog sled." The camp cookbook also mentioned efficient menu planning—drawing a chart and establishing columns of meals: dinner, breakfast, lunch, snacks, and a column for staples and miscellaneous items. Then fill in for each meal of each day the exact amount of every item required.

I snickered to myself and continued reading aloud to the donkeys. "Chicken livers on a skewer . . . Fresh cream. . . Spices needed: anise, fennel seed, dill weed, vanilla extract, red chile sauce, soy sauce, curry powder, dried tarragon leaves...

"Lunch suggestions: beef tartare; deviled eggs; salads of greens, meat, and cheese. Dinner suggestions: hekka to be served over hot rice with Chinese cabbage; Korean beef with mushrooms, cabbage salad with sesame seeds and ginger root; lamb curry (cream style) accompanied with sweet potatoes, chilled dry white wine, and fresh fruit."

I snickered again and looked over my camp food supply: 4 cans of peas, 4 cans of corn, 4 cans of pork and beans, 2 cans Vienna sausage, 2 cans Spam, 2 cans tuna fish, oatmeal, flour, baking soda, shortening, dried apples, coffee, salt, pepper. No butter (melts), no syrup (leaks), and encourages armies of stinging red hot ants to attack camp.

The donkeys never complained about my plain pancakes. Tradition demands that jackass prospectors share their pancakes, which also lures the pack animals in for breakfast and saddling.

During frontier days rugged mountain men and prospectors were at times forced to eat the hides of their trapped furs, crickets, prairie dogs, vultures, mules, crows, mountain lion, or coyotes. Ruxton said, "Raw intestines wound spirally upon a stick and sucked in like spaghetti." Meat's meat, a common saying in the mountains.

I loaded the battered old pannier boxes to hang on the donkeys' packsaddles with dented blackened coffee pot, 2 pans, 2 tin plates, 2 tin cups, 2 gold pans (when not panning used for donkey water and food dishes).

One necessity was an accurate spring scale. In *Horses, Hitches, and Rocky Trails*, Joe Back writes, "Balance the two sides of each pack, being sure they weigh the same, whether they're panniers, side packs of any kind, mantied cargo, bedrolls, tents, or any daggoned ordinary pack you load. And say, Bud, you'll be surprised how much of a liar the scales make you out to be, no matter how good a guesser you think you are. Then hang or sling these balanced loads on the saddle at the same height . . .

"A pack animal has to be packed as comfortable as possible, and still carry a pay load. His burden should be carried on top of the sides of his rib cage, not too far back, not too far forward, or you'll hamper his action . . . If you pack your load too high and too far back . . . the pack will sway and weave too much, won't go far before it slips . . . Quite a few times I've seen potatoes, busted eggs, kitchen hardware, torn up blankets, and other needfuls, scattered along a trail and hanging to tree limbs and snags.

"If you pack your load too low, you will squeeze his torso and hamper his breathing machine . . . you may end up pitching your camp ten miles short of where you figured on going."

I sorted and weighed the outfit and almost tossed the *Cooking For Camp And Trail* into the trash bag, but I thought, "might be useful for fire starting or emergency TP, or if I find Smilin' Jack's gold mine, or a ledge of azurite veined with dendritic gold, then I could afford an extra donkey to carry the spices, fresh fruit, and chilled wine, and even maybe hire a cook to prepare the rabbit borracho simmered in dry red table wine.

Willy edged close to me and grabbed the straw hat off my head and trotted away, Shaggy wheeled and went after him in pursuit of the straw hat. Usually I recovered the chewed up hat before it was hopeless, but this time I was too slow. Shag tried to tear the hat away from Willy and it ripped into a ragged half. (Now I'd need to find my moth eaten felt hat.) Both donkeys munched on their hat pieces; their idea of a camp and trail snack.

## DESERT WINTER

### San Simon Valley and the Peloncillo Mountains

> On a Christmas Day
> we were mushing our way
> over the Dawson trail.
> Talk of your cold
> through the parka's fold
> it stabbed like a driven nail.
> If our eyes we'd close,
> then the lashes froze till
> sometimes we couldn't see...

Uncle Wayne's eyes sparkled reflecting the flickering campfire light while he recited one of our favorite Robert Service poems. He knew by heart; The Cremation of Sam McGee, "There are strange things done in the midnight sun by the men who moil for gold." And The Shooting of Dan McGrew, "A bunch of the boys were whooping it up in the Malamute saloon . . . When out of the night, which was fifty below . . ."

We sat near the campfire, built not so much for heat but as a hypnotic centerpiece. Something to stare at on a still winter night in the Chihuahuan Desert.

Our camp looked over the San Simon Valley. At sunset I saw the hunched fuzzy shapes of the creosote bushes, the Chiricahua Mountains cut into the crimson desert sky. The donkeys eyes luminous like wet fire agates.

Uncle Wayne said, "Up north this time of year I'd he shoveling ten feet of snow. The frontier placer miners dug tunnels in the snow to their workings and built fires over the frozen ground."

Uncle Wayne put his coffee cup down and stood, pulled at his mustache and in his Shakespearean voice boomed, "THE SNOWS WHERE YOUR TORN FEET FREEZE, AND YOU WHITTLE AWAY THE USELESS CLAY, AND CRAWL ON YOUR HANDS AND KNEES, CLEAN MAD FOR THE MUCK CALLED GOLD, .. ERE THE FIRE WENT OUT AND THE COLD CREPT IN AND HIS BLUE LIPS CEASED TO MOAN, AND THE HUNGER-MADDENED MALAMUTES HAD TORN HIM FLESH FROM BONE."

I laughed and slapped my leg, "BRAVO! BRAVO!" Then we howled at the moon like timber wolves, Willy and Shaggy brayed.

"I sure wish we hadn't lost our gold wheel and solar charger, darn! That dust devil just dropped on us like a bomb; sucked up the wheel, 12 volt motor, battery, solar panel, coffee pot, and tin plates fifty feet in the air, then dashed them to the ground. Every time we prospect here something weird happens."

"Yep," Uncle Wayne said, "Last time all our food disappeared and the time before that we found our water cans tipped over and empty."

I picked up the dented, lidless coffee pot and poured us both more coffee. The chipped tin plates were piled with red beans and green chile. Between mouthfuls I said, "Legend claims prospectors were ambushed by Apaches every quarter mile of this wash. You'd think we'd learn to stay out of here. There might be gold here, but six inches or so beneath the surface it's not dry enough to dry wash, and no running water for high banking."

I moved forward and refilled my plate. "I'll miss that Gold Magic wheel. We could work three days with five gallons of water. I even had that inverter rigged up to the wheel's charger to use the typewriter at base camp. Durn!"

Uncle Wayne filled his plate again and said, "We still have our trusty metal detectors, let's nugget shoot and look for treasure some of these dead prospectors stashed before they got scalped."

"Sounds good to me, Uncle Wayne."

The donkeys, ears forward, followed something soundless moving in the chaparral. We'd see things in the desert at night that we couldn't identify. The donkeys saw things. Sometimes they'd get spooked, sometimes the just watched. In the land of Cochise, ghosts pass through – once flesh and blood, now shadows.

I whispered, "Uncle Wayne, there's something out there."

"FOR GOD'S SAKE JILL, WE ARE IN DEAD MAN'S GULCH! OF COURSE SOMETHING'S OUT THERE."

We listened for awhile, and watched the donkeys radar ears. Then it vanished. The feeling gone. Empty space. Willy and Shaggy turned, walked away and munched dried bunch grass.

"Guess we won't be seeing much of our old pard, Klondike Mike," Uncle Wayne said.

"Uh huh," I mumbled. "I know it. Got that post card last week from Mexico, him and Sandilee married. WHOA! I about fell over backwards."

Uncle Wayne laughed and slapped me on the back. "He asked you to marry him about one-hundred times. You wouldn't so he found someone who would."

I sighed and said, "Marriage is like a gilded cage, those on the outside want in, and those on the inside want out."

Uncle Wayne cleared his throat and smoothed his white mustache and recited his version of Robert Service's poetry:

"Have you wandered in the wilderness, the sagebrush desolation ... have you roamed the arid sun lands through and through?" He gestured theatrically at our surroundings. "Have you camped upon the foothills and known the great white silence." He lowered his voice above a whisper. "Ye who take the lone trail, bid your love good-bye; the lone trail, the lone trail, follow till you die."

"Good night Uncle Wayne."

"Good night Jackass Jill."

# THE
# OTHER-HOLE-IN-THE-WALL-GANG
## Carson National Forest, New Mexico

I entered a twenty-five foot long crack between the hanging wall and foot wall. Beyond the keyhole was bright sunlight.

Uncle Wayne and I left the donkeys tied, while we searched for water and a good campsite. Out in the open we couldn't have a campfire, too dry and windy. But if we found a sheltered cleft in solid rock, we wouldn't need the single burner stove which used one-pound disposable propane bottles.

We were southwest of Tres Piedres, named for the three giant granite boulders. These odd shaped rocks are great examples of spheroidal weathering. The granite here in the Tusas Mountains is rosy colored from feldspar minerals turned reddish from decay.

This range is cut by many faults, and made up primarily of Precambrian granite and white quartzite, with outcrops of purplish sedimentary rock.

Somewhere nearby (according to our gem and mineral collecting books) the granite contained bands of coarse pegmatite with pockets of large crystals or books of mica, both black biotite and white muscovite; and good specimens of beryl, garnet, and tourmaline.

Mica rich pegmatites were mined when sheet mica was used for windows. Then in the 1870s after glass became available the mica was used for stove doors.

The Carson National Forest map showed over thirty mines, mostly inactive, within a few miles of where we stood. And according to my New Mexico Bureau of Mines and Mineral Resources map 15, a few miles north are Precambrian vein and replacement deposits of gold and silver. Plus rumors of lost mines and treasures; the Spanish Queen, the Jealous Frenchmen, Jesse James . . .

I emerged into a little canyon, patches of dry grass, and scattered juniper and piñon with shallow prospect holes full of clear water. Shelves of silvery mica reflected like mirrors, palm to tabletop size. A box canyon with only one narrow but walkable way out. I rushed back to find Uncle Wayne.

I unsaddled Shaggy and led him to the rock crevice. Could he squeeze through? I started in slow, letting him sniff and think. He followed stopping a few times to duck down.

"Good boy Shag. Good boy, that's it, no hurry. Good boy." In one low place he dipped his belly and crawled a few feet. I heard Willy's worried braying outside. If Shag got through Willy would follow. I yelled back, "OK Uncle Wayne we made it." He unsaddled Willy and led him into the portal. By removing the donkeys packs and saddles, they'd slide through tight places like dogs going under a fence.

We released the donkeys to roll, graze, and drink while we dragged the panniers, saddles and gear to our secret canyon. Then we walked around, picked up some rocks, and inspected the diggings.

Uncle Wayne asked, "How in the heck did these miners get equipment in and out of here?"

Later we found what looked like hand forged tools – picks, sledge hammers, small hand drills, and smashed shovels. The wood handles long since rotted. No evidence of drill holes for explosives.

I said, "Probably a two man pick and shovel operation. They got in and out the same way we did."

Uncle Wayne called us, "The Other - Hole - In - The - Wall - Gang." Our plunder was thirty pounds of book mica, a handful of beryl crystals, and old tools.

This was our last expedition together until next fall. I'd load the donkeys and start a summer job mining the pockets of tourists somewhere, and Uncle Wayne to his ranch and diggings in the Okanogan country.

Uncle Wayne would keep about everything he found, and I'd sell everything I found. In my case a matter of survival.

"This beats flipping burgers or waiting tables."

"Amen." replied Uncle Wayne.

## PUEBLO SPRINGS, NEW MEXICO

I met my nephews at the Albuquerque Airport. The boys dressed in pith helmets and safari suits, spoke to me in fake Aussie accents; ready for adventure in America's Outback.

We drove singing and laughing to basecamp in Magdalena, 6,600 feet elevation. Basecamp this year was a one-hundred-fifty year old rented adobe house, only one-hundred-twenty-five dollars a month. I couldn't believe my luck. The large windowed room facing the highway housed Buffalo Girls Trading Post, a part-time second hand business I set up to support the donkeys, myself, and our expeditions. All these modern conveniences did take some getting used to— light switches that worked, hot and cold water out of a faucet, and indoor plumbing.

"Guys," I said, sitting up straight, feeling proud, "When we're at base camp, we can 'take a dump' indoors."

We packed and weighed the camping gear, brushed, hoof picked, and saddled the donkeys. I rode Raymond, a tall white gelding. Lane, thirteen, rode Johnny Mac, a stout swayback white gelding. Eleven year old Evan, rode Shaggy, my trusty bombproof spot gelding. Willy, a feisty neurotic gray gelding carried the panniers and top pack. Lane commented, "Why can't we drive a Range Rover?"

I explained again, "The best treasure hunting locations are places four-wheelers can't reach, even a Range Rover, besides that I can't afford one."

Uncle Wayne "horsetraded" for the white donkeys before he went north to his mine in the Okanogan Highlands. The "new" donkeys, both over twenty (middle-age in donkey years) were trained to light harness work, team driving, packing, and riding. I picked them up after the Tusas Mountains expedition. According to Uncle Wayne's instructions these donkeys were for sale or trade; though I'd grown attached to the dusty old gentlemen.

"But Uncle Wayne," I whined into the telephone, "I can't sell them now, they're part of the herd!" This was going to cost me.

We rode a few miles north of town, through Pueblo Springs Ranch. The owners are friends and allowed us access.

Somewhere out here were Pueblo Indian ruins. The springs historically well known not only to the Spanish, but to the Piros, Pueblos, Navajos, Gilas, Mogollons, Apaches, and Comanches.

According to local accounts the first discovery of silver in New Mexico was at Pueblo Springs in 1863. The sites of South Camp, Middle Camp, and North Camp spread over the sides of these mountains. Pueblo Springs had a post office established as Magdalena Mines. The 1880 census listed 47 male residents; 36 reported their occupation as miners, nine as laborers, one blacksmith, and one physician.

In 1883 the post office at Magdalena Mines closed and all mail was sent to Kelly, a boom mining town three miles south of Magdalena whose population grew to over 3,000.

We dismounted and scoured the hills above the springs, and saw a few potsherds and arrowhead chips. This lead us to the ruins. The ancient village had over one hundred rock dwellings built in rows like motel rooms, and two large circular pits. Antelope, deer, elk, bear, wild sheep, maybe even buffalo ranged here.

The Spanish in their search for gold and silver may have captured and scattered these people.

This Pueblo Indian site wasn't on any published map. A local hidden treasure.

We stayed a few hours, let the donkeys graze, and poked around with long "snake" sticks, and picked up a few souvenirs.

I tightened cinches, a boost up for Evan; mounted we moved north crossing ravines and deep washes. The steep banks brought gasps and delighted screams from Evan.

I yelled back, "Lean way back going downhill, lean forward going uphill. If it's too scary, get off and walk."

The saddles creaked and soft unshod hooves clicked on rock through the hot smell of crushed sage. We rode past rock mounds and tipi circles. Indian sign diminished, and we saw a few frontier graves and prospect holes.

After stops to retrieve dropped canteens and to pee, the glitter of scattered purple glass, metal tubs, and lard cans, lead us to North Camp.

Beyond the next hill were the dumps and workings of hard rock mining. A rotting windlass frame hunched over a deep shaft.

"Okay boys, this is it. Unsaddle and water your animals. We're camping here tonight."

Lane jumped off Johnny Mac and walked away. Evan slid off Shaggy, plopped down and groaned, "My butt's so sore I can't move. It's too hot! I'm hungry."

I barked orders, "Lane get back here and take care of your donkey. NOW! Evan get off your butt, unsaddle your animal. MOVE IT BOYS!" They did.

After camp chores I said, "If you want to do some exploring, grab your hard hats, flashlights, and canteens, and we'll check out some of these tunnels and shafts."

We climbed to the top of a waste rock dump to the tunnel portal. "Wait out here while I check this one out. If something happens remember what to do. The donkeys know the way back, just give them free rein, and go get help." I stooped to enter low packed gravel and rock portal, lots of shored up places. The air was stagnant. The hair on my scalp and back of my neck prickled and I heard the dead air whisper, "Get out."

I emerged and squinted in the blazing sunlight. The boys were busy rolling boulders down the dump slope. "We can't explore that tunnel, it's full of rat traps, let's go look at the other ones."

Most the tunnels here were rotten and the airshafts collapsed or filled with waste rock. Only one short tunnel was solid rock with a nice breeze. We could hole up in there if it got too hot or rain clouds rolled in. But tonight we wanted to camp out and listen to crickets and coyotes, see the stars, tell creepy stories, and have a piñon pine fire.

In ore sacks bulging near the tent, we collected about fifty pounds of galena, a lead and silver ore, and about twenty pounds of sphalerite, a zinc ore. Tomorrow I'd get another one hundred pounds of specimen grade galena, which sells to tourists for three to five dollars per pound.

This extra hundred pounds would be slung and packed on my riding saddle. By using the horn and cantle just like the bucks on a pack saddle, and the saddle strings tied to keep the sling from slipping over the cantle. As Joe Back would say, "Tighten up your cinch and prepare to walk, Buddy . . ."

## SAN MATEO MOUNTAINS

The granite columns loomed like feudal fortresses above us. This cattle worn trail wound through a widening canyon. The monochrome landscape shifted to banded rhyolite walls, and green and white striped rock (maybe serpentine and quartz veins) that plunged and folded with dramatic mineralized intrusions. I began seeing evidence of a frontier settlement: corroded tin cans, broken bottle glass, smashed metal buckets, porcelain shards . . . One quarter-mile further through junipers and past a small mountain of waste rock, stood a sagging head-frame, a dismantled stamp mill, piles of bricks and kiln structures; maybe a small smelter and mill site. Old silent machinery, splendid monuments of enterprise.

Shaggy and Willy stopped. I dismounted Shaggy and loosened his cinch. The donkeys turned, huge ears pointed back over the trail. For the last two or so miles we'd stop and look back. Even with binoculars I saw nothing, but I felt someone or something watching, following. I wasn't merely paranoid, because the donkeys also paused and watched our back trail.

A coyote? Mountain lion? Ghosts? Surveyors? The donkeys didn't appear nervous so no use worrying. I patted the .38 revolver on my hip.

My eyes feasted on the rugged rusty grandeur, a pictorial tribute to the power of optimism. My first instinct was to rush around and find a good dumpsite to dig up and sift through the treasure screen (an 18"x 26" wire mesh on a PVC pipe frame with folding legs, which was balanced and tied to Willy's top pack). I envisioned gold rings, priceless coins, gem grade minerals, a small leather bag of gold nuggets, better yet a trunk full of Spanish gold. The names: Jackass Jill, Willy, and Shaggy make world news—but in a few hours darkness would drop, making firewood gathering, tent erecting, finding water to replenish the water cans, and taking care of the donkeys, dangerous near unmarked shafts.

According to the topo map a spring and stock tank was less than a half mile southwest of here. The pipes once brought water to town long since corroded. The presence of range cattle guaranteed water was somewhere. Jake, a rancher, near the Arizona, New Mexico border, ran thirty-five miles of black plastic pipe, some originating from his homestead wells. Other cattlemen, like Roy, his father and grandfather laid over fifty miles of pipe in the last one hundred years. Spacing water tanks over rangeland spreads the cattle out and brings wildlife into unwatered areas.

I unloaded Willy's top pack, panniers, and packsaddle, and unsaddled Shaggy. The donkeys stared behind me, watching, waiting. I looked but couldn't see or hear anything. I spoke to the donkeys, "You boys let me know if it's something important, I've got to set up the tent and gather firewood." I tethered, watered and grained both donkeys. Usually I alternate, one donkey loose, one tethered; but not tonight.

I dropped an armload of wood by the newly constructed fire ring when Willy snorted, flung his head up and down and started braying. I stood up wiping my hands on my jeans.

From behind a waste rock pile a sixteen hand black mule with a white muzzle walked into view and the rider said, "Whoa Belle!" The man wore a brown battered felt cowboy hat and a handlebar moustache. A canvas bedroll behind the cantle, metal canteen, dusty roping saddle, rifle in scabbard, worn boots; a mirage materialized from a Zane Grey novel.

We stared at each other, he looked as though he was stifling a laugh. I said, "Nice looking molly mule. Is she friendly?"

"Yes, Ma'am. Belle is friendly. How about you?"

"Sometimes," I said.

He dismounted, dropped the reins, loosened the saddle girth, took off his gloves and walked a few steps toward me. "Howdy Ma'am," he tipped his hat. "My name is Joe Packer, saw burro tracks. I was checking on my cattle. Ain't seen burro tracks up here in twenty-five years, I was curious, followed them." He glanced at my pile of gear. Four-man tent, shovel, cot, lawn chair, one gallon blue enameled coffeepot, bean pot, frying pan, carrots, potatoes, onions, canned food. "You camp in style."

I invited him for coffee and asked about the water situation. He said two hundred feet away a water valve was under a wood plank. He had extra fittings, clamps and hose stashed at the spring tank. Said he'd fix it tomorrow so I'd have water, close.

"My grandpa was a miner here. He lived right over there." He pointed to the remnants of a rock wall. "When the mine closed he started raising beef. 'People gotta eat,' grandpa said. My brother and me inherited the ranch. He lives in the main house with his wife and kids. I live in the ranch hand's cabin."

I asked, "Is this townsite part of your ranch?"

"Nope, our boundary starts about three miles west, in the valley. We have the grazing rights here."

I told him I was treasure hunting and mineral collecting. He said that sounded interesting. He collected arrowheads. "When I was a kid, about forty years ago or so, my brother and I played cowboys and Indians up here. I know where the garbage dumps were, and the outhouses, stuff like that. I'll show you if you're interested?"

I made dinner and he watered and hobbled his mule and put his bedroll by the campfire. He used his saddle blanket for a pillow. The dying fire hissed and popped. I fell asleep on my cot dreaming of purple bottles, cobalt glass, gold coins . . .

## BURRO, DONKEY, MULE OR ASS?
### Coronado National Forest, Arizona

Shag and Willy stepped daintily out of the stock trailer at the trailhead in the Coronado National Forest. The next two days we'd search for the ghost town of Chiricahua City, Texas Mine, Chicago Mine and Mill, and Hell Lode. The town site and mines were established in 1879 and 1880. Then called the California Mining District, Arizona Territory, in present day Cochise County.

This route followed an ancient Indian trail. The cavalry, Cochise, miners, emigrants and outlaws passed this way. A great treasure hunting location.

As I lashed down the final top pack on Willy an SUV with sightseers stopped next to the two donkeys and myself.

One of the ladies with a Boston accent said, "This is why we came out West. We've seen real cowboys, Indians, and now a gold prospector. And mules! Oh, my; wait until my friends hear about this." The cameras clicked, the film rolled. I took pictures of them with the donkeys. They took pictures of me with the donkeys.

"Yes," I said, "We have bears, mountain lions, ten foot long venomous snakes with heads bigger than shovels. Yes, I've heard of prospectors dying of thirst when their trusty donkey pawed the ground and opened up a spring seep."

The tall balding man asked, "Have you found any gold nuggets?"

"Not yet, I just started looking." But I didn't tell them there was little placer gold here, but mainly hard rock silver. And on this expedition I was looking for century old toilets to dig up and search mine dumps for odd mineral specimens. I did not want to spoil their romantic notions.

She said, "Those are such cute mules. I didn't know they could be so colorful."

The short dark haired man said, "But they look quite like burros, although they are much too large."

"The terminology," I replied, "is confusing. I took a deep breath and began my long rehearsed spiel to the most asked question: What are the differences between burros, donkeys and mules?

"Burro-donkey-ass, they are all the same animal. Donkey is the common name used. Derived from 'dun' (the prevalent gray color) and 'ky' meaning small; though size and color have little to do with it. The Spanish equivalent of donkey is burro.

"The term 'burro' is not considered 'proper' when referring to Mammoth or large jackstock or to the Miniature Mediterranean donkey. The American Donkey and Mule Society uses the term burro only when referring to feral animals, and those sold through the Bureau of Land Management." I paused and petted Shaggy. "You'll find a kind of East-West division in the term use, too. In the West most mid-sized donkeys are labeled burros as habit, but not in the East. Kind of like the Texas way of calling all young horses, colts, even fillies."

I checked my audience for signs of boredom, they appeared rapt, so I continued. "'Jack' is the proper name for the male ass. Jackass is also proper, but the added ass is not necessary. 'Jennet' is the proper name for the female ass. Jenny the informal name.

"A jack," I continued, "is crossed with a female horse (mare) to produce a 'mule.' Mules are considered sterile hybrids because the unequal chromosome numbers don't pair up and divide properly.

"A mule can be any height. A mammoth donkey (called Mammoth Jackstock) bred to a Belgian or Percheron mare will give you a working mule about the size of a one-ton pickup truck. A Miniature donkey bred with a miniature horse or pony will give you a mule about the size of a Labrador Retriever. A gelded male mule is called a John, a female a Molly.

"If you see an animal that looks horse-like, but the ears seem large compared to a horse, it's probably a mule. If the equine has large dominant ears, no withers," I pointed to the place right under the front bars of Willy's packsaddle, "pot belly, small neat hooves, and a scrawny cow tail, the critter is probably a donkey.

I petted Shaggy's neck and said, "Shag is a spotted large standard donkey. Willy is a gray-dun large standard donkey with the typical dark cross over his shoulders and stripe down the center of his back, which you can't see well because he is fully loaded with camp gear."

I waved good-bye and added, "Now if you meet a donkey aficionado and she or he owns a Miniature donkey, you can safely say, 'You have a nice small ass.' If he or she has a large tall donkey, you can state with confidence and conviction that, 'You have a great looking mammoth ass!'"

## DRYWASHING
### Rodeo, New Mexico

I sat next to John on a bar stool at the Rodeo Tavern. I argued, "Winter and early spring is the best time to drywash. My drywasher isn't equipped with a blowdryer to dry the dirt." John sipped his Bud Light looking skeptical, his fingers and teeth nicotine stained. His mule skinner hat battered and sweat stained.

He looked me in the eye and said, "Woman, the only time to drywash is during the summer. You need hot air to create static-electricity, you can't recover gold any other way."

"But," I said, "July and August is the rainy season, can rain everyday. You can't drywash mud." I paused, took a sip of my Guiness Stout. "Summers should be spent at high elevations near cold streams sluicing for gold and gems." But I knew true desert rats, like John, scoff at this and are seen in arroyos at high noon in 110 degree weather, with assortments of gold recovery apparatus: 12 volt drypanners, drywashers, propane or engine driven dryers, metal detectors.

"You're a wimp," John said.

"Your brain is fried," I replied. We both laughed and ordered another round.

John said, "Me and my partner were running two engine driven drywashers on BLM land near Prescott when a forest service water truck and fire crew descended on us like a swat team to put out the 'fire.' Seems our dust was reported as a fire from the lookout tower. The crew boss told us to cease and desist operations until proper permits were issued. Although he had no idea what permits we needed." John took a sip of his draft beer and sucked in deep on his non-filter Camel and continued, "We knew from experience it would take months to get an answer. That's why we worked on BLM land. Usually they left us alone. Two old men with drywashers. Hell. One dust devil moves more ground than we can in a week!" He took another drag on his cigarette. "So I went to the fire tower with a fifth of whiskey and got the lookout guy to agree to ignore the dust clouds from our operation. Took care of that problem."

He ordered another beer and I sipped on my dark beer. I said, "I mined in Idaho with a portable stream sluice. A college kid, seasonal forest service guy, stopped and watched. He measured and timed my little stream of silt. I asked him if he was joking. And told him he ought to follow the bull moose that just waded by. You could still see the mud where he pulled up plants. But the guy was serious and wrote down numbers in his notebook. I laughed so hard I fell on the river rock and rolled around. I think I ticked him off, because two days later he came back with official paperwork for a permit."

I took another sip of beer. John cussed and stamped out his cigarette. I continued. "The season was too short, no time for bureaucratic stalling. A permit to run that dinky sluice, a cupful of material at a time? So I said 'heck with that!' loaded the four donkeys with tents, shovels, buckets, food and sluice box and packed two miles up an unnamed creek to a ghost mining camp. Aspen, fir, and pine trees grew into the road. Inaccessible even to a four-wheeler."

I paused, bought us both another beer. John sat silent, smoking and I continued. "I worked for the forest service up in the Okanogan National Forest on a landline survey team. No forest employees I knew except the survey crew and timber cruisers walked more than one-quarter mile from their rig. I figured if I made camp a couple miles from any road I could work the season without getting bothered by the silt police. The donkeys acted as perimeter guards. They heard moose, deer, elk, coyote, fox, bear and one bobcat before I could spot them with my binoculars. Never saw a human for two weeks. Found some nice gold, too."

We laughed and clinked our glasses. John leaned over and whispered, "My buddy bought one of those stealth dredges for prospecting and I rigged up a twelve-volt drywasher with a solar panel charger."

"I always wondered how those things worked?" I asked.

"We have to keep the batteries charged, but we don't have to haul fuel in. We see lots more wild animals. And I can hear a truck coming two miles away."

"Cheers." I said and we clink our glasses together again.

John sipped then took a drag on his cigarette. "We even got scrutinized on our own claim last year. Someone reported engine noise. A real hassle. More paperwork."

"Well, I'll be damned," I said, "We have the silt police, the dust police, and noise police."

"You forgot one," he said. When you go prospecting with your donkeys you'll have to start packing a rake and garbage bags."

"What for?"

"The turd police."

"No shit?"

"No shit."

## SILVER!

### Granite Gap Mine

I pried the boulder off the heap of backfill in the abandoned drift. Doing this exposed a substantial mound of silver ore. "I knew it! I knew it was here somewhere!"

A study of the oxide ores at Granite Gap made by Phelps Dodge stated, "The major metal of interest in the district was silver . . . and chemical analysis of several 'pure' galena fragments showed silver values in the range 100-150 oz/ton. In most of the workings, oxidation has occurred as deep as mining has pursued the ore. There is little doubt that oxidation enhanced silver values, most silver now appearing as chlorargyrite. Selected ore samples taken in well mineralized structures commonly run 100-500 oz/ton silver."

When I read: "500 ounces per ton of silver," I nearly fell off the rock I sat on. I jumped in my truck and drove to Rodeo RV Park and Country Store, seventeen miles south of the mine, where my friends Marianne and Ed (and their nine children) own and run the store, park, and fuel station. They had the village's only copy machine.

I fired out a copy of the Phelps Dodge report to Uncle Wayne, and scribbled a side note; "PS: Mountain lions have killed all the bighorn sheep, and a bunch of Jake's calves. Bring me a rifle. All I have is this .38. Thanks. PPS: Another rancher said he saw a jaguar about five miles southeast of here while checking his cattle, and Jake's mare spooked at something and threw him, he busted some ribs."

Uncle Wayne and his mining buddy, Samsula Pete left a phone message at Rodeo RV Park saying, "We are on our way south. See you in a week or so."

I was planning to extract from the depths of that mountain all the hidden treasure! On the instant my temperature rose five degrees. Yes, I had silver fever; like gold fever and malaria recurs without warning.

I loaded the donkeys with tools, lights, water, and they dragged the ladders up the mountain trail. The silver deposit had to be one or two levels above the ore stash.

A postcard note sent by Pete and Wayne said we needed to wash the tunnel walls and back in mineralized areas to see anything. During blasting even a century ago the fly rock and dust covered every exposed surface in the mine and would belch out the portals and ventilation shafts. So I brought a whisk broom, and some spray bottles of water.

I knew better than to climb around alone, but waiting for Wayne and Pete drove me to pacing and wringing my hands and eating large quantities of chocolate bars. My heart pounded, I couldn't sleep, and when I did I dreamt of silver bars. I convinced myself Uncle Wayne would stop in every mining district from Oregon to Colorado; it might be weeks before they arrived and by then I'd be dead from seizures anyway so I might as well die hunting rather than die waiting.

I always brushed out the tunnel portal floor the first ten or so feet just to see the tracks of critters who ventured in. Usually civet cat, ringtail cat, bobcat, javelina, birds, snakes, coyotes, an occasional lone male coatimundi, and desert bighorn sheep (before all were eaten by lions.)

I unpacked and unsaddled the donkeys at the Big Labyrinth mine portal; gave Shaggy and Willy some water and grain and staked them out. They acted skittish and weren't very hungry. I thought maybe they sensed my malarial agitation.

I dragged a pannier full of tools into the tunnel and I paused to glance at the tracks. Large round pads, Newfoundland dog size, claw marks absent. Feline. A very large feline. Now, I felt skittish.

According to my *A Field Guide To Animal Tracks*, and *Mountain Lion Field Guide*; lion tracks are round with the claws normally retracted. A cat has a trilobal heal pad, distinguishing the track from a large dog or wolf. Cats walk neatly and leave a straight trail. The front foot tends to spread the toes more than the hind foot. The mountain lion front foot print is about 3 inches in length and 3 ½ inches wide. The hind foot 3 inches by 3 inches. My Field Guide To Animal Tracks has a measuring scale on the back cover; these prints measured 5 inches by 4 ½ inches. I felt the hair on the back of my neck prickle, a cold chill sensation crept over my body.

Jaguar, the largest species of cat in the western hemisphere. Larger head, heavier body, and shorter, thicker legs than the leopard and mountain lion. Usually yellowish to buff with black spots, but the subspecies sighted was a dark phase with subdued spotting. The jaguar has a distinctive roar, like true lions. The cougar or mountain lion (not a true lion) does not roar. Its vocalizations range from whistle-like, snarl, hiss, low growl to a shriek or scream.

This gave me the heebie-jeebies, and I tried to talk myself out of it by saying, "Well, it's just another big cat, lot's of food wandering around, maybe it just ate one of Jake's fat calves and won't find plump human and donkey meat tempting. This was vexing. A mountain of silver waited while I stood here talking to myself.

"DAMN THE TORPEDOES. FULL SPEED AHEAD!" I quoted loudly.

I let the donkeys go. Willy and Shaggy could amble back where Raymond and Johnny grazed. Four donkeys could fight off a lion two maybe not.

I checked my weapon, packed flashlights, batteries, candles, matches, water, whisk broom, spray bottles, ore sacks, sledge hammer and chisels; gloves, hard hat, rope, and emergency flares which scare away most wild animals. I carried this stuff and one aluminum extension ladder into the drift where I believed the silver horde waited. My mouth was dry, and I was plenty afraid. My bowels started to rumble. I hoped I wouldn't get a case of scours.

The clatter I made should irritate sleeping lions and make them go away. Or maybe the jaguar was guardian of silver mountain and I would die a horrible death trying to extract the treasure.

I found a small stope to extend the ladder and climb to the next level. I felt weak and shaky, but I searched for hours, whisking away grit and spraying water on rocks looking for the silver lode. Then it happened. As the water struck the ledge the metallic luster was unmistakable. A shot of adrenalin made me tremble and sweat while I fumbled for my tools. I chipped and chipped, and hammered and hammered at the three foot thick vein. The pile of silver ore at my feet grew.

I sat down and drank some water. I must have fallen asleep because I woke suddenly and cracked my head on the wall. My hard hat had fallen off. I opened my eyes but I couldn't see. It was solid blackness. Where was I? What happened? My body felt like it fused to the rock. I couldn't move. Then I saw lights reflect and bounce off the walls, and a clang on the ladder, and I drifted back into blackness.

"JILL! DAMMIT JILL! WAKE UP."

I tried to speak but no sound came out. I was being shaken. I mumbled and squinted up into the dim light. Then I felt a slap on my face. In a raspy voice I said, "Leave me alone." And I tried to swing at him and he caught my wrist.

"Well, thank God," he said, "You'll live."

I was so stiff I couldn't move. I rolled over on my stomach and tried to crawl. "Oil. I need oil. I think I rusted like the tin man.

Uncle Wayne laughed and asked, "How long have you been up here?"

"Gee, I don't know. Five or six hours, maybe."

"BULL!" Uncle Wayne snorted. "What DAY in the week did you come up here?"

"Early this morning, Monday." I replied.

"Jill, guess what? It's Wednesday."

"Oh."

Then I heard a whistle and nearby a man crouched by the pile of ore I chipped out. "This looks like high grade material you have here." He threw Wayne a chunk. "Heavy. Real heavy."

Uncle Wayne turned the flashlight toward my face. "You ought to see yourself. You look like you've been wallowing in a mud hole for a month."

I looked at Uncle Wayne, he was slightly dusty, but his face clean and his white hair a little wild but his blue eyes clear. Then I stared at who I knew must be Samsula Pete. Short cropped light brown hair, graying, and a neat trimmed beard. His dark, friendly eyes looked amused. I tried to brush down my hair with my hand, but it was stiff and matted. Hopeless. Something in my stomach stirred, but I knew it was not scours.

They looked me over again and at the silver vein in the wall and we all burst out laughing. "WE'RE RICH! WE'RE RICH! WE HIT THE MOTHER LODE."

## RODEO TAVERN

This was our second trip up the steep trail today. The donkeys hauled water, food, and recharged wet cell batteries for the miners lights. I unloaded this stuff at the portal and made two wheelbarrow trips six hundred feet into the mine drift and dumped the load at the base of the ladder. At first I climbed the chained together ladders two levels above the main drift with gunny sacks full of supplies. Sick of that, I rigged up a rope and pulley system. I could hear the muffled clang, clang of the men's sledges on steel, but they never heard my shouts below. A whistle sometimes worked;

the solution, a large cow bell dangling off the hoisted baggage. Then I carried the empty water cans, discharged battery packs, garbage, and sacks of silver ore to the mine portal where the donkeys waited patiently.

This tunnel was too narrow and snaky for the donkeys with full panniers. An ore car and tracks would be nice, but all the steel was ripped out in the 1940s for the war effort.

Frontier style mining was tedious. Uncle Wayne and Samsula Pete had chipped out all the exposed silver ore, mainly galena and chlorargyrite, and did some minor blasting.

Pete said, "See these blebs in the sphalerite. The matildite blebs and platelets form these nodules, some of considerable size. These," he assured us, "are highly collectible and worth the painstaking hand chipping and drilling." Uncle Wayne groaned. Pete continued, "These are worth far more intact than spot price for smelted ore."

As they worked and chipped and drilled, when I wasn't hauling supplies to the men, or cooking, I searched for firewood. I gathered and used up every stick of wood within a half mile radius but was remedied by the great abundance of bois de vache or cow chips.

I took the dull drill bits and chisels to Ed in Rodeo to grind and sharpen, and batteries for charging. Our generator had choked, popped, and quit running. The parts were being shipped from Chicago. Last year it took two months for new valves and valve guides to arrive and they weren't the right ones. This generator, even if it did run, was too big to haul up the steep mountain trail without a helicopter.

Instead Shaggy and Willy hauled a Honda 1000 watt generator strapped to poles in a stretcher between the two donkeys, rigged like a travois except the rear donkey had the pole ends secured to his sides at girth level, sort of a "push-me-pull-me" arrangement. But the small generator could not deliver enough power through 800 feet of cable to run the battered air compressor. Erratic air pressure and stall outs jammed the expensive bits into solid rock.

Lots of water was hauled by the donkeys (Shaggy, Willy, Raymond, and Johnny Mac) to cool the quickly dulled drills. Drilling dry would create what Uncle Wayne called "death dust". Finding this silver lode and becoming rich was getting depressing.

After working 14 hours a day for three weeks, we decided to go out and eat a giant pizza at the historic Rodeo Tavern. This turn of the century high beamed adobe building was the meeting place for cowboys, ranchers, and miners, when the trail drives ended here in Rodeo's railroad stockyards, and mines shipped ore to El Paso. Rodeo a border boomtown, now quiet but still alive with ranchers, farmers, tourists, and a few miners drifting in.

Rob Bernard, the tavern owner greeted us and took our order and asked how things were going at the mine. I told him, "Hitting the mother lode isn't all it's cracked up to be. They docked us real bad at the mill for the lead. Plenty of silver, but the spot's so low."

A stocky dark haired man walked to our table from the bar, and introduced himself as Ramone Guerro, said his grandfather was a superintendent at the Granite Gap mine from about 1897 to 1903. "My grandfather heard one of the owners, a hombre named Pratt, was closing the mine. So grandfather started dumping half the high grade into an abandoned rock chute below the main level. Grandfather and three other Mexican miners were going to buy the mine, but there were lawsuits and the United States and Mexico Development Company bought it and later it was sold to the Hartford Insurance Company from back East. Grandfather Jose Guerro died in 1915. He always wanted to buy that mine."

Uncle Wayne said, "You're welcome to come up any time, and we could always use another partner or investor."

Ramone shook his head and laughed, "I'm just a farmer, I know nothing of mining, but I will stop. I haul chile and cotton past Granite Gap every fall, I will stop."

Pete said, "Have a seat. Join us for pizza. We need somebody here doing something worthwhile, making money from the land, we certainly aren't!"

We all laughed, lifted our drinks for a toast; Uncle Wayne's bottle of dark beer, my glass of burgundy wine, Ramone's shot of tequila, and Samsula Pete's mug of root beer.

The days trudged by. We all talked about finding Jose's ore stash, but didn't have time. The silver ledge pinched out, and the men drilled, blasted, chipped, and searched. Two months of slave labor yielded three tons of medium grade ore. I remarked it was a good thing we didn't borrow money to finance that ore crusher and processing equipment, over one-hundred fifty thousand dollars.

Samsula Pete warned us about debt. Sometimes he was practical to the point of irritation. Pete said, "We might have five million dollars worth of ore here, but if it takes five million to get it out, we've got zero." He was right of course, but still irritating.

Uncle Wayne lost interest in our old glory hole and spent time poking about in the vast maze of tunnels, lowering himself with ropes into every shaft and winze searching for Jose's high grade cache.

Samsula Pete helped me load the one ton truck with ore for the mill site in Arizona. This small local mill wasn't supposed to dock us so hard on the lead.

Today was the big barbecue at Granite Gap. After dumping the ore I was bringing back a half cord of mesquite, twenty-five pounds of ribs, and five bags of ice. Pete was digging a new outhouse hole and tidying up. We hadn't seen Wayne all morning. Ed and Marianne with most of their nine children, Ramone, and whoever else wandered in would be here about 2 p.m. In winter it got dark early and cool at night, but the warm daytime sun and evening bonfire made border winters perfect.

"Where in the heck is Uncle Wayne?" I kept asking Pete.

He didn't know. "Hadn't seen him all day."

The barbecue was well under way. We all pigged out; smoky mesquite, juicy ribs, beans, potato salad. At five o'clock the sun was setting. The landscape on fire in deep orange glow. Then darkness. The fire yellow, flickered and popped, casting shadows. I was worried now.

"Let's go find Uncle Wayne. I know it's easy to lose track of time in a mine tunnel. But Wayne does not miss barbecues. Something must be wrong."

## UNCLE WAYNE
## AND THE LABYRINTH MINE

Uncle Wayne tied a bowline knot to a log stull above the shaft. Grasping the safety line he climbed down the rickety wood ladder. Falling rock or equipment had knocked some of the rungs off.

He poked around this unexplored drift looking for the high grade ore stash Ramone's grandfather dumped a century ago. He used one hundred feet of line to get here, and had another one hundred feet left.

He'd go back soon because his stomach growled just thinking about the mesquite barbecued ribs, and potato salad, waiting for him down at basecamp. What time was it anyway? He just snagged his watch on a square nail, it clattered down here somewhere. Maybe he'd find it.

He explored this level awhile, looking through muck piles for the ore and his watch. He followed some ore car tracks till they ended at a rock walled ore chute where ore was dumped to a lower level for storage or into waiting ore cars that miners pushed or pulled to the landing for sorting and shipping by way of mule drawn ore wagons. "Maybe, just maybe, this is it," he said to himself.

Near the top of the chute an anchor bolt protruded from solid rock. Wayne kicked the bolt and decided it should hold his weight. No ladder here. He'd use his climbing skills.

He laughed to himself thinking if Jill were here she'd complain and say something like: "You're like a monkey. I'm jealous I can't get to places you can; I've got the climbing grace of a bovine. I'm the ground level gopher. And you're older than me! It really ticks me off!"

Then he'd reply, "If you lost forty pounds—"and she'd throw something, usually a cow turd, at him. He chuckled to himself while he tied off, double checked his gear, leaned back and stepped down the rock chute

At a small ledge about 50 feet down, he stopped and braced himself, fumbled in his shirt pocket and lit a match. Was the flame yellow? Would the flame stay lit? The air felt fresh and cool, but he wanted to make sure.

This rock tube banked and sloped downward and reminded him of a Disneyworld ride. He pointed his headlamp to the bottom. Was it 35 feet farther or 40 feet? He had rope left. Should be enough, he hoped. He lowered himself till he was five feet from the end of his rope.

He twisted around to look down, his foot slipped and his hard hat and light fell off and dangled from the battery pack on his belt. The line slid in his hand, and as he grabbed with his other hand, he felt the end of the line slip by. He had forgotten to tie a knot in the rope end. "Damn."

In total darkness his slide felt like a scene in slow motion. His forehead banged against rock and he started to go backwards when his feet hit bottom. He folded and collapsed.

He thought to himself, *I probably fell only ten feet*. He didn't feel anything, yet, just numb and surprised. The only sound was his panting and his heart beat pounding in his ears. He yelled out a few times. A futile gesture. The rock walls muffled the sound anyway.

His head started to ache and his right hand burned. He groped in his backpack; still intact; candles, matches, flashlight, extra batteries, a canteen, candy bars, and toilet paper. He could probably get the miner's light to work again, change lamp bulbs or something.

At basecamp the campfire glowed. Everyone mentioned how good Wayne's secret barbecue sauce was. The cookout a great success. Marianne and most of her nine children went home. Her husband, Ed, and son Andrew stayed to help. We worried about Wayne so we organized a search. Pete suggested we take all the line we had, two water cans, the wet cell battery packs and headlamps, flashlights, and dry cell batteries. Pete, Ed, and I would search for Uncle Wayne. Ramone volunteered to stay at the campfire with Andrew, just in case anyone else (including Wayne) showed up.

I put the packsaddle and panniers on Shaggy. We filled the boxes, slung the 400 feet of miscellaneous rope on top, and headed up the trail to the tunnel we called the Big Labyrinth. Poor old Shaggy. A heavy load for one donkey. I should have saddled Willy or Raymond too, but Pete was so impatient, he wouldn't wait.

On the mine trail there was much excitement, worry, and nervous joking.

I walked behind Samsula Pete leading Shaggy. I watched him, like countless other times. His dark piercing eyes; often critical, a perfectionist. He talked amiably with Ed. Ed a retired mathmatics teacher and physics major and Pete, a structural steel draftsman (when not mining); both precise, but Ed's nine children and cheerful wife long since wore the hard edge off Ed's personality. Although Pete seemed sensitive and intensely curious. He asked lots of questions, charming questions. But I felt like a specimen he was dissecting. He teased, he was funny, but despite all that I never felt warmth.

"Pete, did Uncle Wayne have his flask with him?" I asked.

"He better not have. I told him specifically I did not appreciate him using any type of alcoholic beverage while working."

"Oh," I said, "I sort of thought he might share. In fact I wish I had a toot right now." Pete shot me a disgusted look.

Soapy, our new mine dog ran up ahead. This blue heeler female showed up about a month ago. Neck and ear torn and bloodied, and her body emaciated. The first thing she found to eat was a bar of soap. Uncle Wayne and I fed her and cleaned her wounds. She was supposed to go to the dog pound in Lordsburg, but we never got around to it, although Pete volunteered to take her. Soapy did well here. She never fell in any shafts.

At the tunnel portal we dropped the line and un-slung the panniers. I loosened Shaggy's cinch and tied a twenty foot lead to his halter. We donned hard hats and buckled on our battery packs. Pete carried 200 feet of rope and Ed took the other 200 feet. I put canteens, flashlights, candles, and first aid stuff in my pack.

Soapy sniffed ahead. "Soapy, where is Uncle Wayne? Go find Uncle Wayne!" I said in a sing-song high pitched dog lovers voice (which I knew Pete hated).

We passed shafts and wood ore chutes, twists and turns. We yelled, we whistled, and Soapy barked. Then we stood still and listened.

In a cavern like stope Soapy climbed to a limestone shelf that dropped off on the other side. We kept walking, checking winzes, raises, and shafts, but Soapy wouldn't budge. She stood at point, not moving, though we called her. So we scrambled up the loose rock to Soapy and the ledge which separated the two open stopes. This cavern linked to another level.

We followed Soapy into this twisty drift that was only three feet high in some places. The tunnel opened up again, and on the left was a shaft with an old wood ladder, and the log stull above the shaft had a rope tied to it.

Soapy whined and wagged her tail. We yelled and whistled, but heard nothing in return. Pete climbed down while Ed, myself and Soapy waited. He yelled up, "Lower the longest line if I need it."

A half hour later I heard Pete's whistle, so I lowered a long line and let it drop.

About an hour later we heard voices below and lights bobbing. Uncle Wayne emerged with a scraped and bloody forehead. Soapy flapped her tail and pawed at Uncle Wayne. Pete about ten minutes behind brought Wayne's pack. Said he left the line below for further exploring.

Uncle Wayne said, "Let's get out of here! I'm starving." Ed and I reloaded Shag and we walked down the mountain in darkness, laughing, our lights dancing off the limestone and rhyolite boulders. Soapy dashed ahead chasing a jackrabbit.

At camp Uncle Wayne and I took sips from his flask. We made a promise and a toast. "No more traipsing around any hole in the ground alone." Pete and Ed agreed. We all feasted again, then Ramone took Ed and Andrew home. Soapy had a heap of rib bones to work on and Shaggy crunched on a large scoop of grain.

Pete brought ore samples from what we called "Uncle Wayne's Lost Mind," for testing before we went off again in frenzied pursuit of riches.

## LOGGING IN THE ZUNI MOUNTAINS
### Summer 2000

We climbed, sweated, and grunted to the Continental Divide in the Zuni Mountains. The tangle of Gambel's oak and spindly juniper meant hard travel for myself and four laden donkeys. The saddle horn on Shaggy kept snagging on overhanging limbs, and the wood panniers on Willy and Raymond got wedged between trees. Johnny Mac's canvas packs caught on branches. Each stuck donkey waited patiently while I went back to loose them from the grasp of these creepy trees.

Despite this I found sea fossils in limestone and Mancos shale; the donkeys unshod hooves crunched over cinder cones. We passed other-worldly volcanic domes and lava tubes, and plodded through acres of what looked like semi-polished agates where conglomerate rock eroded and released a tumbled palette of multi-colored banded, solid, opaque and transparent pebbles. Jasper, onyx, chalcedony... I halted here to gather about fifty pounds of these rocks for final polishing.

Donkey hooves clicked across tilted slick-rock and we pushed through more brambles. Discouraging. "Durn!" I said to the donkeys, "I left the Northwest to get away from this. Stuck in trees again! Sorry guys."

Uncle Wayne suggested I go north with him to his ranch and gold mine in the Okanogan Highlands for the summer, "Cause you're not doing anything important, you don't have plans?" True. But there was something about the Southwest . . . I wasn't raised here, but when I moved here it just took me in and I knew I couldn't stop living under this naked brazen light. I didn't need the islands, year round snow covered peaks, or the towering trees anymore. I needed the emptiness, the skeleton of the land jutting up exposing its past. Moonlight over granite.

The Continental Divide follows the Oso Ridge through the Zuni Mountains. The Zuni Mountains range from 7,300 feet to 9,500 feet elevation. The Continental Divide is sort of obscure here, these mountains are not jagged and dramatic; nevertheless, it marks between west-flowing Colorado River drainage and east-flowing Rio Grande drainage. Flanking the Zunis are distinctive salmon-pink striped Zuni sandstone bluffs and erosion carved weird pinnacles and balanced rocks.

We meandered through aspen groves and flushed flocks of Merriam's turkeys, camped on ridges backed by large ponderosa pine stands, and pushed again through shrub oak, Rocky Mountain maple, and sumac. And made good use of abandoned railroad beds and overgrown but passable logging and skid roads.

*The road had the merit of all savage trails, and of all the tracks a man still makes who is a-foot and free and can make by the shortest line for his goal; it enjoyed the hill.* – Hilaire Belloc, *The Old Road*

I hunted for treasure in several ghost towns and logging camps. Steam railroad logging in the Zuni Mountains began in 1892 and ended in 1942. Log cabins of the early 1900s dot remote canyons and hillsides near creeks and springs. All my digging in dumps and outhouses yielded only a few purple bottles and some silverware.

Grass for the donkeys grew thick in Water Canyon, Bonita Canyon and in the aspen grove canyons. At 8,000 feet the daytime temperature reached 70 degrees, but the dishwater still froze at night.

I saw mule deer and elk herds, mountain lion tracks, and granola like bear blob the size of cow flops.

Each time my donkey packstring attempted crossing a driblet of running water, I faced rebellion and mutiny. Luckily Shaggy and Willy, longtime veterans of waterlogged Washington and Idaho expeditions, swam across rivers and tiptoed over bridges above steep canyons and raging rivers. Despite their experience, Shag and Willy still leapt over spring seepage and nearly dry creeks as if some hideous serpent lurked in the water molecules ready to rip their guts out.

At the edge of a two inch wide "creek," Raymond and Johnny Mac stopped as if a solid wall of writhing copperheads materialized. The whites of their eyes shown in mute terror as I pushed and pulled. Even when I hitched Shaggy and Willy together and they pulled while I pushed, these desert born donkeys wouldn't budge.

103

I gave up and pitched camp on the opposite side of the "creek," made coffee and thought how I could winch them over.

In training Shaggy and Willy, I sometimes used a block and tackle to cross moving water. That was years ago. Raymond and Johnny Mac had only seen puddles of water after occasional rain showers, and these puddles were suspect and given a wide berth.

I leaned back, sipped coffee, found a pencil and began writing in my spiral notebook another chapter in *The Adventures Of A Donkey Prospector*.

After a week of donkey water torture, most the donkey pack train moved through and over water when asked; except Johnny Mac, who remained sullen and uncooperative. So I'd leave him carrying the mineral specimens on "the other side" while we ambled on. I'd eventually stop, unload the donkeys, and give them treats just to get old Johnny motivated, it usually worked. Although one night he didn't get in until about midnight. His load listed starboard. I think he tried to roll, but the canvas panniers, balanced, lashed, and diamond hitched, stayed on.

We followed an overgrown skid road and got caught again in undergrowth. I hated this. "What this place needs is a good fire, preferably not while we're here. Or better yet, well funded thinning contracts."

Uncle Wayne often said, "Thinning gets rid of the pecker wood and eliminates out of control forest fires."

Amen, I said to myself.

Later I saw some faded scraps of survey tape on a branch near an old fence line, most the posts rotted, and a muddy yellow sign smeared with bird poop which read, "Ramah Lake Realty, Located in downtown Ramah," I laughed at this, downtown Ramah was two blocks long. I got out my GPS Unit. It took twenty minutes to get a location fix and by then the low battery warning flashed.

I tried my cell phone and got through to the number on the sign. Cindy, the real estate agent told me the property was "Forty acres, still listed. $20,000., ten percent down. Mineral rights, and timber rights." She continued, "I carried that sign up there two years ago. Everyone said I was crazy; no power, no water, no road."

"Yes, I know I'm standing near your sign now. I packed up here. My truck is down at George's in Ramah getting a rebuilt engine. I got stranded so I'm making the best of it."

"Wow!" she said, "Sounds exciting. I didn't know cell phones worked up there?"

"It's a bag phone. Has more watts or something." I said.

"And," she said, "the parcel you are standing on borders the Cibola National Forest on the south and west sides. Give me a call back if you want me to come up with maps and more info."

I searched for a clearing and Johnny Mac got stuck again. "This place definitely needs thinning." I turned around frustrated and almost stumbled over an old rotten lichen covered log, so I gave it a hard kick. "Ouch!" I about broke my toes. Petrified wood!

I marked the location and we moved on looking for an open flat space to set up basecamp. After finding the first rock log I noticed chunks of fossil wood strewn all over the hillside.

After I watered the donkeys and let them graze I found more petrified wood. More than this pack outfit could haul in one trip.

That evening I rummaged through the wood panniers for my books, a dozen or so reference books and a few paperback Westerns, and found the six-hundred page text – *Minerals of New Mexico*.

PETRIFIED WOOD: wood replaced usually by a cryptocrystalline silica form of quartz. This silicified wood generally chalcedony, jasper or agate (which is considered variegated chalcedony). This wood

is called by many names, primarily distinguished by coloration: Agatized wood, jasperized wood, wood agate and combinations thereof. "Salicified wood occurs also in Triassic rocks of the Zuni Mountains . . . Some of this wood represents the same species of conifer that is so abundant in the Arizona Petrified Forest . . ."

"Hi. Cindy. I'd like to put earnest money on the forty acres. I called Uncle Wayne, my partner, he said OK."

She said, "I'll be up in two hours. I can four-wheel in part way, and hike the rest. See ya.."

Shaggy, Raymond, Johnny Mac, Willy and I "logged" that property. And we filled a storage unit in Ramah. For that summer anyway, we were the Zuni Mountain Hard Rock Loggers.

## SOAPY AND THE BLACK BEAR
### Zuni Mountains

For two months the donkeys skidded and packed out about a ton of petrified wood, and a few railroad and logging camp collectibles. The pack train halted often, snagged in underbrush.

I missed mining camps and barren desert, but the most annoying was the bears.

Where would I sell the petrified wood anyway? The Arizona and New Mexico markets were saturated. Every rock shop had at least an acre of the stuff for three to five dollars per pound. But still a nice forty pound piece could sell for two hundred dollars.

Finding the fossilized trees was exciting. According to one of my text books, the trees fell and were covered with silt, mud, and volcanic ash, which cut off the oxygen and slowed the logs decay. Then over time (a long, long time) silica-bearing ground water seeped through the logs and replaced original wood tissues, and this silica crystallized into quartz.

The color of most the natural petrified wood was muted and I had trouble distinguishing wood from rock. But sometimes minerals and impurities were deposited while the wood was petrifying which added bright colors and interesting patterns.

Another curious thing, the logs often looked as though a woodcutter with a chainsaw bucked the logs into stove size rounds and left it to rot. Supposedly, after the trees were fossilized (sometimes three thousand feet underground), the Colorado Plateau emerged. This uplift caused pressure against the logs which broke into segments.

Another reason for leaving (besides the bears): logging camps, even villages with thirty to forty large permanent log structures showed little or no evidence of the barroom and brothel. Families lived here. Few whiskey bottles. Quiet, peaceful, tidy. I called these places "minimal treasure recovery sites."

Albert D. Richardson wrote in *Beyond the Mississippi*, "All mining districts have a mysterious family resemblance." Among them rusted heaps of mining equipment, whiskey bottles, beer buckets, discarded and intact medicine and perfume bottles, lost rings and coins . . . anything but quiet, peaceful, tidy.

I also needed to pick up Soapy, my spotted blue heeler, her stitches healed and removed. After chasing numerous bears away from our camp and food stash, she harassed an ill tempered bruin. Normally bears left quickly or climbed a tree, when a dog nipped at their heels. This one did not.

I didn't see the battle, but I heard it. The thick underbrush and darkness made it impossible to help her; except firing a few shots in the air, and banging pans to scare the bear away. She eventually dragged herself into camp. I encased her ripped body in two rolls of blue vet wrap to hold her guts in and I wrapped her in a wool blanket and tied it with baling twine. Her eyes burned wild and red.

At first light I placed her in a large pannier box slung on Shaggy. Her body trembled, her eyes now dull and feverish while she watched me load the off side pannier with water jugs, food, battery pack, and cell phone to balance her weight. She was in shock, probably dying.

I left Willy, Johnny Mac, and Raymond in the polywire corral on the mountain. Shaggy carried Soapy and we walked carefully to the valley below.

I called Uncle Wayne and said, "She's pretty bad. Should I shoot her?" I waited, a lump in my throat. "It's probably going to cost about a thousand dollars?"

"Oh, hell," he groaned into the phone. "Soapy probably saved our butts a few times. Like that day she wouldn't let us in that mine tunnel at Silver Hill? Huge cat tracks? Remember? She growled, her hackles up. And she body slammed me when I tried to get past her! God, I love that dog." Pause. "Then the time she found me when I slipped into my glory hole, the rope dangling out of reach above my head—"

I broke in, "I know, I know, but I didn't think the veterinarian would take petrified wood in trade, although he probably would accept some gold nuggets. The gal at the Real Estate office said she'd take care of Soapy for a while (if she lives) so she won't rip her stitches and drain tubes out—and trade later for donkey rides, her and the grandkids."

This wasn't grizzly country, but the acorns, berries, pine nuts, grubs, rodents, and my camp rations kept the black bears well fed. Even my canned food was methodically punctured by teeth, and the contents lifted and sucked out.

I hadn't seen so many bears since I left Grande Cache, Alberta Canada. The small coal mining town lacked a drive-in theater so some of us spent Friday and Saturday nights parked in pick-up trucks at the dump, drinking beer and watching the bears fight over garbage.

One Saturday, close to midnight (still light that far north) five black bears fought and growled over some chicken bones. Then all five stopped and watched something in the woods. Suddenly bears bolted in different directions away from the dump. Vanished.

A grizzly emerged, quiet as a snake. The unmistakable hump, huge head and dished face.

The only sound was the squeak and grind of truck windows rolling up. Nobody laughed. No beer bottles clinked or lifted. Nobody got out to take a leak. What a majestic and terrifying beast. He sniffed the air. He sniffed the ground, and took a chunk of something and strode soundless into the forest. No other bears showed up that night.

Today was moving day. Our last load. As I lifted a forty pound segment of petrified wood into Raymond's pack he bolted and the boulder landed on my right foot. The pain shot up my leg like a lightning bolt. A black bear strolled by. I rolled around and cussed like a mule skinner. The loud cursing sent the black bear into a lope.

"Well guys," I said as I lay on the ground, "It's times like this I'm glad you're not horses. I'd be trampled and you'd be two miles away; gear hanging from limbs, panniers and tack busted all to heck." The donkeys ignored me and munched on tree limbs, the bear forgotten. Willy had spooked and ran about thirty feet. Raymond trotted twenty feet, his unbalanced panniers and drooping ear made him look drunk. Shaggy and Johnny Mac hadn't moved an inch. I got up and limped around. "I'll live . . . BUT I'M SICK OF THIS PLACE! Let's find us a barren desert."

## ALASKA BEARS

### Summer 1982, Trapper Creek, Alaska
### September 2000, Zuni Mountains, New Mexico

"Dammit, Willy! If you don't get in this trailer, I'll be cookin donkey burgers tonight." Days like this when it's hot and I'm tired, shooting him crosses my mind. After an hour of sweet talking, bribery, and finally inching him into the trailer like a big fish, I shut the gate behind Willy.

A couple years ago I discovered another loading method for Willy. The tents and gear were packed, and all the donkeys (except Willy) had stepped nicely into the trailer, ready to go. I pushed and pulled and cussed for about and hour and said, "Hell with you Willy, you can stay here. A bear or mountain lion will eat your ornery ass!" So I latched the stock trailer gate and drove away. The old flatbed and trailer rattled down the potholed dirt road.

My truck left a trail of dust and I heard what sounded like a fog horn with hiccups. I stopped, put on the parking brake and turned the ignition off. Listening, I heard frantic braying and galloping hooves coming down the mountain. This time when I swung the trailer gate open, Willy hopped right in. This loading technique has worked a few times since then.

I climbed back in the truck and headed south to the desert; away from the trees, tangled underbrush, and the bears. The Zuni Mountains were dry this year, the bears hungry, bold and dangerous.

Soapy, my blue heeler put her head on my shoulder, looked back once at the donkey trailer, rolled her eyes, put her head back on my shoulder and looked at me, disgusted. I swear she said, "Stupid donkey."

I longed for a ghost mining camp with rusted heaps of mine equipment, dumps to rummage through for mineral specimens, and outhouse holes to dig for old bottle, rings, coins . . .

I stroked Soapy's ragged battle scars from the Zuni Mountain black bear. My memories drifted back to Alaska on Cache Creek where I dredged for gold one summer, and camped for awhile with Stan, an Alaska State Game Biologist. He told me lots of bear stories.

One question to Stan was, "What is the difference between the brown bear and the Grizzly?"

Stan said, "Some authorities designate the Alaska Range as the physical boundary. Bears (other than the black or polar) to the north and west of the Alaska Range are called grizzlies, while bears on the eastern slopes of the Alaska Range and southward are called brown bears. But," he continued, "most guides and people like me who spend time in the field studying them consider the brown and the grizzly the same animal. The brown is referred to as the coastal bruin and the grizzly denotes Interior grizzlies. In any case the brown/grizzly is an awesome creature."

Stan also told me these mammoth bears could drag a full grown moose or steer uphill through alder trees. "I'd seen where a moose carcass would hang up, the bear would tear alders out roots and all, just like a skidder dragging a log right through the trees, ripping out anything in the way. Pure raw power."

I threw another log on the campfire, and felt a creepy sensation, like a centipede crawling up my spine. Stan continued, "Grizzly boars will kill and eat cubs. I saw a boar grab a cub in his mouth, jump on it with his forefeet, tear it to pieces, gulp it down, while the sow fought him from the rear and side. He didn't fight her back but waited, lurking around until the sow came into heat. If the cub is killed, she will reproduce the next year."

I refilled our tins with coffee. Stan did not smoke, and did not drink alcohol when he worked out here. He had short cropped light brown hair, glasses, and wore khakis. He looked more like an accountant in delivery driver's clothing than an Alaska game biologist.

He took a sip of coffee then said, "A partner and I a few years back at McNeil River observed a grizzly bear feeding on the remains of another grizzly bear. We darted and tagged the 800 pound sow. A dangerous job. We also checked the stomach contents of the dead bear, we found parts of a fawn and a bear cub."

I threw another chunk of wood on the fire, the sparks flew up. I thought I heard something behind me; the centipede crawled up my spine again. Stan wasn't concerned, so I didn't want to say anything and act like another sissy from the lower forty-eight. To cover my nervousness I said, "I heard that bears don't eat people? They kill them sometimes, and don't eat them. Is that true?" I knew the answer, but I was hoping he'd lie about it or have some boring statistics to make grizzlies less real while we sat in front of this wimpy fire, in the twilight shadows of the midnight sun in grizzly bear country.

"Bears are a lot like pigs," he said. "They're omnivorous, and eat about anything they can find, and even wallow in mud when possible.

"When a bear makes a kill, it usually covers it in a pile of vegetation and dirt to let the meat tenderize. The bear will be nearby protecting his kill from intruders. The bear eats whe wants, covers it back, and returns again and again. I have been involved in search parties along with State Troopers to locate people who have been mauled, injured, or killed by bears. It rarely happens but sometimes there are only enough remains to put in a small sack. Given enough time a bear will break the large bones for the marrow and crack the skull open for the brain. Nothing goes to waste."

In my pack I had a journal with notes from The *ALASKA SPORTSMAN* magazine. I read to Stan something Clark Engle, a guide, said about grizzly bears. "When they start to woof and chomp their teeth, they're upset. That's a very unpredictable animal right at that point—you don't know if they're gonna charge you, run off or just chew up everything that's around. I hollered to the hunters, 'He's back! Don't breathe; don't move; don't do nothin!'"

The vivid daydream of my crushed and bloody skull in the jaw of a griz ended when Soapy whined and scratched my arm. We both had to pee. "OK, Soapy. I'll find a place to pull over. Thank God we are getting out of bear country, back to more reliable, tangible things like six foot rattlesnakes, javelina, centipedes, scorpions, Gila Monsters, blood sucking conenose beetles . . ."

## STACY AND THE JAVELINA
### Peloncillo Mountains

I rebuilt the fire on last night's coals, and added water and grounds to yesterday's pot of coffee. Two mornings ago I poured a drowned mouse out of the cold coffeepot. Stacy screeched. "It's OK," I said. The mouse is dead." She didn't drink anymore coffee, even though I told her I boiled it real good.

Stacy, a landscape architect from New York, my only paying expedition customer this week; first time "Out West," wanting to do something offbeat. Her tanned skin stretched too tight over a sculpted nose and blinding white capped teeth, and more eye makeup than a raccoon. She wanted to go prospecting, treasure hunting, gold panning.

"Two hundred dollars deposit, and two hundred dollars when you arrive." I had said into the cell phone.

"By the way," she said, "I'm a vegetarian."

The donkeys eyed me suspiciously while I started repairs on the tack. A hole punch, baling twine and duct tape fixed anything. In panniers I packed: gold pans, metal detector, water cans, canned food, coffee, cots, tent, sleeping bags . . .

Cots I believe are a necessity. It's dumb to sleep on the ground by choice when red ants crawl in your ears, and the bloodsucking cone nose Assassin bug, whose poison causes a furious itch, followed by the hives and fever, leaving

a hard itchy oozing sore for a week or two. Yes, you can sleep on the ground like they do in western adventure novels if you want.

I touched up the sign in my outhouse. ATTENTION: Watch out for rattlesnakes, coral snakes, Gila monsters, centipedes, ticks, black widows, tarantulas, horned toads, red ants, fire ants, scorpions before being seated.

The summer rains just ended, lots of pot holes and rock basins had water for the stock and for panning. Although there wasn't much placer gold here, most people wanted a frontier experience, how it felt to crouch over water and swirl a gold pan. I often salted their pans, especially the kids' pans with a few flakes of Idaho gold. Then I could sell the parents a gold pan and a bag of *Jackass Jill's Gold, Silver, and Garnet Panning Sand.*

I dumped a pound of steak sized slabs of ham into the frying pan, and boiled water for her greenish gray whole grain organic breakfast, which looked to me like something obtained from a very sick calf.

"Carnivores and pig meat. Disgusting." she mumbled under her breath.

I explained the dry creek bed full of sand is called a "wash" out West. Rattlesnakes and Gila monsters live in the rocky grottoes along the wash. "Oh my," she said.

She noticed the revolver I carried, and asked why. I said because I might need to shoot something, and she said it would bring bad karma on us.

Stacy had never slept outdoors or experienced any form of primitive conditions, except as she mentioned with pride how well she handled a two hour power outage.

I handed her a roll of dusty toilet paper and told her to go behind those granite boulders, and bury the works under some rocks.

While Stacy squatted behind the boulders, a band of fifteen javelina moved noisily toward her. The donkeys watched the wild semi-pigs. They rooted with their pig like snouts, heavily bristled grizzled hair with a yellowish tinge on their cheeks, some with large tusks. They snuffled while feeding.

Willy the donkey became irritated, head low, ears flattened, he charged the band of javelina. Stacy screeched and she hopped, clutching her pants like in a gunny sack race, to our camp and fire.

The wild pigs sounded a barking cough alarm, scurried off about a hundred feet, then turned and looked at us. The odor behind the granite boulders was irresistible to the scavengers and they ambled back to our toilet area and cleaned up everything, paper and all.

I turned to Stacy and said, "Nothing goes to waste in the desert."

I added more sticks to the fire, reheated my coffee, and boiled water for Stacy's calmative herb tea, which I thought, looked and smelled like horse turds. She asked about the Desert Bighorn Sheep that ranged here according to a New Mexico Magazine article she read.

"Well," I said, "Used to see herds about every week right here, but the mountain lions ate most of them."

"Mountain lions? Oh." Her tanned skin went translucent. She stared at me with fish pale eyes. "Have you ever shot anything?"

"Yes," I replied. "

"Are you a good shot?"

"Fair," I said.

"Good." she said.

When Stacy left her face looked relaxed, her fingernails cut short and sensible. The raccoon eyes gone. She even ate a tiny piece of ham and drank some miner's coffee after she saw I didn't die.

## MICRO-GOLD
### Coronado National Forest, Arizona

Hikers stopped at the mine and showed me a rusty specimen of quartz. It looked like something you'd find in a scrap yard. Some of the best gold-bearing quartz is rusty and ugly.

According to the couple who found the fragment, the area was deeply eroded, exposing an outcrop of rotten quartz. They thought it looked odd and out of place. I traded them a nice piece of malachite with azurite crystals for the quartz piece.

By appearing only slightly interested in their find, I got them to show me the approximate location on my battered well marked Coronado National Forest map.

I hammered the quartz into fragments, and ground it down as fine as possible in an old cast iron pot. I panned it and found micro-fine black and dull metallic dust.

I used a loupe to magnify the minerals, but still couldn't identify them. So I got in my truck with the powdered material and crossed the valley from my mine shack in the Peloncillo Mountains to Jess's cabin and laboratory at the foot of the Chiricahua Mountains. He was a retired microbiologist who loved to look at things like bug guts smeared on slides under the microscope. Jess and his family bought 120 acres here. His other passion was searching for and extracting micro-fine gold.

The metallic glint I saw was almost certainly chalcopyrite (copper pyrite) or iron pyrite, fools gold. I knew if I rotated a questionable sample in the light, its crystal surfaces would wink or change their reflective pattern. Gold specks, being rounded, have a steady, less brassy shimmer.

These mountains yielded primarily silver-capped desert copper deposits. Some of the silver porphry is dingy yellow or greyish-white, resembling the plumage of a street pigeon. Any gold found here, according to most reports, was a by-product of smelting.

Under the microscope the specks loomed. I tilted the slide slightly. Peacock colors shimmered from the chalcopyrite and the unmistakable glow of gold. All I could say was, "Wow!"

Jess said, "Bring down a load of this and we will work on separating the gold."

It took all day to cover only three miles. The donkeys patiently picked their way over the boulder strewn switchbacks and gouged out trail. The days at this elevation were sunny and short and the nights bitter cold. If it snowed we'd have to turn back, and wait until May or June.

I missed Uncle Wayne. He stayed this winter at his Okanogan ranch, because his longtime Canadian girl friend, broke her ankle. Barbara usually took care of the livestock when Uncle Wayne was gone.

Uncle Wayne had spent the last four winters with me in Arizona and New Mexico. Summers busy with tourists; I hadn't time to get lonely, but now I was. I had my dog Soapy and the donkeys; Shaggy, Willy, Johnny Mac, and Raymond. But it wasn't the same. More than once Uncle Wayne said, "You need to find you a man."

And I'd always reply, "But I'm not domesticated and I travel too much."

On the phone one day he said, "Maybe you ought to stay put awhile. See what happens."

Last week I hiked over an obscure trail south of Rustlers Trail where Mexican bandits raided north, Apache bands raided north and south, and gringo outlaws held up stages and pack trains and killed each other; hundreds of frontier mine dumps, and now an outcrop of micro-fine gold . . . maybe there was enough to keep me here. For a while anyway.

## ASSASSIN BUGS

### May 2001, Granite Gap Mine and Rodeo New Mexico

I swam in the warm Atlantic Ocean, when a ten foot long sea nettle wrapped around my body. I woke suddenly and found I wasn't swimming in tepid sea water, but laying on a cot in a mine shack in the Chihuahuan Desert. My hands, soles of my feet, and armpits burned and itched.

A few hours ago I drifted to sleep, the first warm night in spring. I groped for the flashlight then pointed the arc of light to my cot. Five conenose beetles clung to my blanket searching for a blood meal. I squished them all, one spurted fresh blood. I knew I'd been bit, and probably experiencing an allergic reaction.

I tried the cell phone. No service.

Had to get to the trailer and the land line phone. Soapy, the mine dog, jumped in the truck. We reached Highway 80 and headed south toward the village of Rodeo.

I cursed myself for not using the tent. Last week I camped out insect free, this week a different story. I knew better. And I knew I was in serious trouble. The conenose beetle creeps up on you like a stalking cat when you are asleep. Attracted by the infra red of a warm blooded host. The parasite's saliva anaesthetizes the skin, it inserts the stylet of the proboscis into a capillary to feed. You don't feel a thing.

Fifteen known species of conenose live in the U.S..The most troublesome and numerous are found in Arizona, New Mexico, Texas, and California. Also known as kissing bugs or Haulapai tigers and are members of the family Reduviidae, which are commonly called assassin bugs. Conenoses are in the genus Triatoma which are bloodsucking parasites of domestic and wild animals and humans. The conenose adults are ½ to 1 inch long, brownish black, broad, flat, nocturnal insect whose wings form a distinctive "X" when folded. It has a cone-shaped head and resembles an elongated tick after an uninterrupted blood meal.

The conenose beetle can carry a protozoan which causes incurable and sometimes fatal Chagas Disease (a form of African sleeping sickness) in humans. The protozoan is not directly transmitted during feeding but is excreted in their feces. If the fecal material is scratched into the bite or onto mucous membranes, it can enter the human body. It is important that bites are washed to remove fecal matter. Also conenose beetles feed on woodrats and mice.

Robert Matheson writes in *Medical Entomology*, "When a bloodsucking insect bites, it is always possible that the proboscis may be contaminated with pathogenic organisms. If such organisms become localized near the point of puncture or gain access to the blood stream, results may be serious. It is always wise to use some disinfectant such as alcohol, tincture of iodine, etc., and to press out the blood if possible, from bites made by insects" I knew this but the bites were all over my back, and I couldn't do anything about it. One insect can inflict numerous bites due to a disturbance during feeding, which causes the insect to reinsert its proboscis.

I hunched over the steering wheel, willing myself to keep driving. I hadn't seen another vehicle and I didn't expect to. My body was covered with burning welts, and I was weak and nauseated. My mouth tongue, larynx, and trachea swelled.

I remember reading in *Poisonous Dwellers of the Desert*, that people repeatedly bitten (this being my sixth time) can develop severe allergic reactions, whose symptoms may lead to anaphylactic shock, vascular collapse, unconsciousness, and death.

My persistent thought and concern were the animals. Who would take care of my faithful donkeys; Shag, Willy, Johnny Mac, and Raymond? Would they be auctioned off and slaughtered, or worse yet left alone in a small corral, crippled from overgrown hooves? And Soapy, the watchful mine dog? Would she look dolefully out the chain links of an animal shelter? Would anyone know their stories, or care?

I pulled up to the locked green stock gate and stumbled out of the truck. Now I was sweating, my vision blurred, and I doubled over from stomach cramps. I fell to my knees and fumbled with the lock. Thank God it wasn't a combination lock. I drove through and closed the gate behind me using a rock as a stop.

The dirt driveway leading to the trailer and phone was only a quarter-mile long, I was almost there.

Soapy secure in her yard around the trailer, full self-feeder, overflowing fish pond and the donkeys with plenty of brush and weeds to eat and an automatic fill stock tank.

I slid the glass door open and fell into the living room and felt my way to the phone.

Months ago, someone at the Rodeo Tavern told me if I called Portal Rescue, a volunteer team of EMTs would arrive in ten to fifteen minutes, but a call to 911 went to Lordsburg over fifty miles away, could be an hour before help arrived.

I started to punch numbers. I knew Portal Rescue's number, last digits 2222. But I misdialed and got someone who thought it was a crank call. My voice did not sound human. Finally I hit the right numbers and heard the words "Portal Rescue."

I crawled to the toilet and evacuated my bowels; I'd probably pass out and did not want to foul myself. A few minutes later the phone rang, but I collapsed before reaching it. A voice on the answering machine said, "The ambulance will be there in a few minutes."

My body was paralyzed. I could not move, speak, or see; but I could hear everything. Soapy barked, the yard gate unlatched, the glass door slid open. I heard soft comforting voices and the sound of velcro pulling apart. A radio dispatcher talked. The donkeys brayed wanting treats and attention. I smiled at this. I felt fine now. Light, euphoric, ready to float away. Both my arms were held and probed and heard things like, "I'm searching for a vein. Any luck that side . . . I'll have to probe . . . collapsed . . . I don't like this BP. . . need to transport . . . hospital . . . 50 miles . . . should we heli-vac? Anaphylactic shock . . . semi-conscious." Someone patted my leg and said, "You'll be alright."

The metallic clang of the transport gurney extending and locking. The wheels turning, moving into dark night air. Radio dispatch voices clicked off and on. Then the stretcher sliding on metal, snapping into place, brightness, doors slam . . . siren, my bed swaying comfortably.

When the probing found a vein, and the IV liquids dripped into my blood the light euphoric feeling was replaced by heat and intense nausea, my head ached worse than any migraine I ever had, but I could see blurred shapes and lift my head slightly.

Epinephrine, Benadryl, and other treatments I couldn't pronounce brought me out of shock, and I shakily left the hospital the next day.

I rigged up a mesh tent over my bed and put my bedding inside. I checked the other tent closely for tears and packed it in the donkey pannier, and bought a one man nylon tent to put behind the truck seat.

"Next time you get bit," the doctor on duty said, "you will have about ten minutes before you become unconscious, then die. The ambulance and EMTs will not get to you in time."

Now I carry an EpiPen to inject myself with epinephrine and keep Benadryl liquid and capsules with me.

Uncle Wayne had a saying, "We are all three minutes away from death . . . try holding your breath for three minutes?"

Soapy wasn't sent to an experimental laboratory, and the donkeys didn't end up in cans of dog food. "So," I said to Soapy while she flapped her tail in the dust, "We all escaped death another day. Where shall we search for gold and treasure next? Let's see." I unfolded the battered topo map. Hmm . . ."

## DEAD MEAT
### Summer, Granite Gap Mountain

Shaggy and Johnny Mac brayed outside the mine shack's doorless entry. Last week a dust devil ripped the open door off its hinges and dropped the mangled mess about three hundred feet down the arroyo. I hadn't got around to fixing it.

Usually at dawn, instead of a rooster crowing, all four donkeys would bray quartet fashion into the doorway demanding their morning ration of hay cubes. Soapy barked and nipped their noses, keeping them outside and away from her dog food.

The sun hadn't struck its fiery glow yet, so it was comfortable. "Good morning boys," I said to the donkeys. "Where are your buddies Willy and Raymond?" Shaggy stood trembling, and Johnny Mac stared at the hill behind the shack. "What is wrong with you guys?"

I wasn't concerned till I saw blood streaks on Johnny's white chest and neck, and crusted blood on Shaggy's nose, forelegs, and girth.

I snapped leads on their halters, gave them moistened hay cubes and inspected their injuries. They nibbled at their food, obviously not hungry. I washed Johnny Mac's and Shaggy's wounds. Mostly scratches, not real deep. "Thank God."

Soapy paced around whining. She smelled last night's drama. "I wish you guys could talk."

I unfastened their lead ropes. Stuffed them in my rucksack with two quarts of water and extra ammunition for my .38. "Let's go Soapy. We've got to find Raymond and Willy."

Shaggy followed. Johnny Mac stayed at the shack nibbling the hay cubes. After we crested the hill I heard what sounded like distant braying.

I remembered the diagram of the horse's head, with the X drawn from the base of each ear to the opposite eye. You shoot holding the muzzle of the gun ¼ to ½ inch from the spot where the lines intersect. This insures a clean, humane death with one shot. The truth is I shoot twice, just in case, and I always feel sick to my jugular, let the blood drain then butcher. Otherwise, buzzards, ravens, coyotes, and insects feasted. I pictured this to mentally prepare myself for the worst.

My plan, a nice uneventful day, sitting in the shade next to the water trough, with all four donkeys nearby swishing their tails, while I cleaned mineral specimens to sell and pan the black sand I got sluicing in the San Francisco River in Arizona. The gold I found there was deep golden coppery color, grainy and about rice size. Some of the prettiest placer gold I'd seen—second only to the wire gold I sluiced from Swauk Creek in Washington State.

My rendezvous in two days with Texas Jack, helping him run a dredge on the San Francisco River would have to wait, "Oh, the plans of mice and men," I mumbled to myself.

Shaggy and I followed Soapy into a ravine and wash to an outcropping of limestone and ancient ash. I saw Willy standing guard, tossing his head and pawing the ground, throwing a dust cloud all around him; his eyes wide, the whites showing. He saw us and trotted over, braying frantically. Then I saw Raymond on the ground.

Raymond was a white roan and the coagulated blood red was unmistakable.

"Damn!" I gasped.

Willy pushed me repeatedly with his head and just about knocked me over as I approached Raymond.

Raymond was the most calm and gentle donkey I had. Guiltily, I wished it was Johnny Mac, my most sullen and humorless donkey. But, I sighed, life does not work that way.

Raymond's appearance was not that of death. His body didn't sag into the ashy ground; no hoards of droning flies, no buzzards with fresh strips of red meat.

I got on my knees, stroked his neck, and talked to him gently. He even lifted his head a little and brayed weakly. I checked his gums. Still pinkish. Good. He perked up a little, and his eyes lost the glazed-over look. It appeared his left flank was deeply gored, and his back and neck were covered with bleeding scratches.

Back at the mine shack I had livestock grade penicillin in a cooler, and a vet kit with iodine crystals, needles, syringes, large curved suture needles and dental floss for field stitching.

I took the hard hat out of my pack and removed the head liner and dumped the two quarts of water into this makeshift plastic bowl, propped Raymond up, and dunked his soft muzzle into the water. He drank long and deep. Good sign. Very good sign.

I looked closely at his wounds, deep scratches and bites. Nearby in the powdery ancient volcanic ash were unmistakable tracks of a struggle between equine and large feline. This mysterious cat is

known by many names: puma, catamount, panther, mountain lion, cougar.

But the ultimate challenge. "How do I get you out of here old boy? Can't leave you here like lion bait."

I snapped a lead on Shaggy and we walked the half-mile to the mine shack for supplies. Willy followed us part way, but trotted back to Raymond when he heard him braying.

I made a quick call from my cell phone to Texas Jack's voice mail. Canceled the mining expedition and explained the situation. I had a very bad kitty here at Granite Gap.

Johnny Mac stood in the shade. When I approached him with a lead in my hand, he trotted away. "Jerk," I said to myself. "Go ahead, stay here alone." So I loaded Shag with water, medical supplies, tent, matches, axe, dog food, donkey food, my food, and we left.

Willy stood near Raymond munching on a stick. He trotted toward us with the stick still in his mouth. "I see you're getting firewood for our night vigil. Thanks Willy."

I poured more water for Raymond and gave him some soaked hay cubes to keep him occupied while I check his injuries. I put salt in a quart of water and rinsed his exposed wounds with this. Then dropped iodine crystals in another quart of water and flushed the wounds again. After assessing the injuries, I squirted 10cc syringes of penicillin into the long claw wounds, and into the puncture wounds. The gaping flank gash needed stitching. I dipped the floss and needle in iodine and began. I got three seam stitches in before Raymond attempted to lurch to his feet. I left the needle dangling.

He did not have the strength to rise on his own, so I braced myself and tugged forward on his halter. He staggered to his feet swaying and shaky. "Good boy, Raymond, good boy, steady boy, steady." I unsnapped Shag's lead and clipped it to Raymond's halter. If I let go, Raymond might fall. So I left the medical supplies, tipped hard hat, water can and bottles scattered on the ground. I'd get those later. "Can you walk boy, one step at a time, good boy, good boy. Let's get out of here."

I took pleasure in picturing the lion's head blown off with a high powered rifle (which I didn't have), although I knew I'd feel a little sad seeing that beautiful wild thing dead. Ranchers get compensation for predator killed stock (although not near enough or often enough) but I get nothing. The cat must die. Big cats hate dogs and usually stay away from their yapping. The donkeys would be safer near the mine shack and Soapy.

Raymond staggered and lurched toward camp, dragging his hind leg, the needle and thread dangled, the stitching job unfinished. We got within one hundred feet of the cabin and Raymond went down. I felt lucky to get this close.

I brought Raymond food and water, got two more stitches in, clipped the floss suture and squirted more penicillin in the still gaping wound. Then covered his hindquarter with a piece of cotton sheet fastened with duct tape and sprayed the works lightly with insect repellant. This would have to do.

Texas Jack left a message on my voice mail, "I'll be there with a couple rifles, soon as I can."

Texas Jack took Shaggy and Soapy and tracked the cat. The next night I heard the distant crack of a rifle and its echo off Bighorn Sheep Mountain. The following morning Texas Jack, Shaggy and Soapy walked into base camp. The carcass gutted and skinned, draped and lashed over Shaggy's sawbuck packsaddle.

Later he scraped and worked a salt and alum solution into the hide. He said some of the hide and skull were damaged. Seems the donkeys put up a good fight. An ear was torn, patches of fur and skin ruined, teeth knocked out, lower jaw broken. "This lion would have died anyway," Texas Jack commented. I cut and boned the meat of the large male cat, and placed the strips into bowls and pans and covered all the meat in a brine of salt and black and red pepper. Then I placed the meat strips on a cotton sheet atop the shed roof, and draped another sheet over the meat; all of this anchored down with rocks, and left to dry in the hot sun. Not exactly fine cuisine, but as the mountain men would say, "meat is meat."

We pulled Raymond to his feet, and led him slowly to the shaded side of the shack for his convalescence. We retrieved the door, rebuilt it, and straightened the hinges. Dredging for gold would have to wait. Oh, the plans of mice and men.

## POLLYANNA'S MOUNTAIN LION

"You actually let someone shoot 'the cougar' at Granite Gap Mountain?" She gasped horrified after she saw the mountain lion pelt stretched and tacked to the mine shack.

"One, of the cougars." I corrected. "Let me show you something." She followed me to see Raymond, the donkey still crippled and scarred from the mountain lion attack.

"Poor cougar, must have been starving, to attack an animal that large!" she exclaimed.

"Nope," I said, "the cat had lots of backfat. In fact my friend Texas Jack and Jake, the rancher, found a steer carcass killed by the same cat nearby with nothing but a bit of haunch chewed on."

She shot a hard glance at me. She obviously didn't believe this. I looked at her and sipped my cold coffee. She wore Lands End bird watching attire, including the binoculars. She quoted and sniffed, "Wild animals never kill more than they can eat."

I almost choked on my coffee. "I have a sheep rancher friend in Colorado who lost fifty-two ewes in one night to a single mountain lion. The record number of kills in one night, one-hundred-ninety-two sheep, happened in Glade Park, Colorado."

She interrupted, "It had to be dogs, only domestic dogs do things like that."

Before Ms. Pollyanna left she commented that it was too bad mining had ruined the once beautiful mountain, although she did buy a few mineral specimens that came out of the mountain. She also had on a leather belt and wore gold, diamond, and opal jewelry. Where did she think all those natural resources came from anyway?

Most people who live and work outdoors; farmers, ranchers, miners and prospectors, have a more practical viewpoint when dealing with predators. We know from firsthand experience a lot of wildlife writing and information is "a bunch of bull corn." I had in fact read, "The coyote is a solitary animal and feeds strictly on rodents, they do not travel or kill in packs." But, I saw twelve coyotes chase and take down a deer? My ranching neighbors have seen packs ranging from ten to twenty coyotes kill full grown range cattle (although they do prefer calves).

Another fallacy often quoted ". . . wild predators only kill the sick, crippled, and old . . . if the kill is left undisturbed, they will feed till nothing is left . . . "

An article by Ben East in *Outdoor Life* chronicles a cougar hunt in Montana involving cougar hunter, Roy Murray. Traveling on horseback in February, he took with him one dog to help him track a particular cat. Murray soon found the cougar's first kill, a two-point buck. Some entrails were eaten. He camped out and the next day came upon a second kill, a big doe. The cat had eaten the liver and little else. The second night he camped out again. The following morning he found the cougar's third kill, a six-point buck mule deer. After a third night out, Murray found the fourth kill, a big cow elk. The elk had a calf but for some reason the cat left it alone. The cat ate only the cow elk's liver. The next day he discovered the cougar's fifth kill, a yearling cow elk. Again he ate just the liver. Later the same day the cat killed a yearling steer. This time the cat ate only beef liver. After camping out another night, he found a yearling doe mule deer. The cat had played with the deer before killing it and ate only the liver and a few bites of the ham. The following morning he found a calf elk with only the liver eaten. Murray's dog tracked the large male cougar to a thicket and chased it to a slab of rock. Murray shot it. Nearby, he found the carcass of a two-year old elk. The cougar had eaten only the liver.

Enos A. Mills recorded his discovery of a "herd of deer, nine in number, that had been killed by a single cougar operating in deep snow." He noted the cougar "had eaten but little of their flesh."

I sorted, repaired, and repacked the tack, mining equipment, and camping outfit. Uncle Wayne would be here within two weeks. Yippee! Uncle Wayne and I talked it over and decided to give Raymond (still limping) and Johnny Mac (sullen as ever) to some folks with a small chicken ranch. Seems a bobcat was decimating their flocks. The donkeys would patrol the grounds at night. Guard donkeys. A good useful job, but still I felt guilty, and I would miss them.

The pack donkeys, Shaggy and Willy; the mine dog, Soapy; myself and Uncle Wayne were meeting Texas Jack at the San Francisco River in Arizona to prospect for gold. This time I'd keep a rifle around, just in case.

## CALIFORNIA DREAMIN'
### San Francisco River, Arizona

Bent over, my face and hands dirt and sweat streaked; I was digging a hole in an ancient river bed shelf above the San Francisco River in Arizona. Shaggy and Willy helped me haul this paydirt to the river for sluicing.

Uncle Wayne was test panning upriver for a better place to put Texas Jack's dredge.

Texas Jack had been dredging with thirty feet of hose, in twenty foot deep sweep holes, never hitting bedrock. He planned to add another ten foot section of hose and go deeper, and had nozzled down his six inch hose to four inches. He said his eight-horse Briggs provided plenty of suction power, but we talked him out of it. He couldn't see down there and nearly got buried in an underwater rockslide.

I remember black out conditions in Alaska and Idaho, twenty-some years ago. I used a ten inch suction dredge (sometimes nozzled to eight inches) in deep holes, ponds, and slow moving water. Working underwater in darkness is a disorienting sensation—like a gut wrenching amusement park ride with your eyes closed. I didn't know which way was up. Then I'd hear an underwater rumble and grating noises, but couldn't see the boulders or rockslides coming. The results sometimes: damaged throttle cables, face masks ripped off, smashed air hoses. Now I prefer a sluicebox, highbanker, or a small dredge in shallow holes close to bedrock.

Texas Jack was rolling up and dipping the miner's moss carpeting from his sluice box into a plastic tub. Nearby was his array of multi-colored plastic buckets, some holding precious black sand. Texas Jack growled at me as the donkeys and I strolled by. He growled again and said, "I see you lusting after my buckets. Don't even think about it." Soapy lay in the sand nearby and whapped her tail. I was referred to around camp as "no buckets." When I slung plastic buckets from Shag's and Willy's sawbuck packsaddles the donkeys invariably crunched the brittle plastic on trees and limbs, dumping the hard earned material on the ground.

Uncle Wayne laughed and said, "Those rascals are doing that on purpose. They learned to scrape trees and dump their loads so they can graze. Then you obediently scramble around on your hands and knees cussing. The donkeys find you amusing and call you a 'dumb ass'." Uncle Wayne was right. After I used smaller but sturdier metal pails Shag and Willy gave up pushing against trees and limbs. Smart asses indeed.

One day the donkeys pointed their big ears at the hill above the river, then I heard a vehicle chug and tires crunch down the steep switchback road to the river. Occasionally people showed up to picnic, fish, or camp. All of us including the donkeys enjoyed these diversions.

A shiny new ensemble of Dodge diesel truck and overhead camper with all the do-dads attached including a satellite dish,

came into view. Uncle Wayne whistled and said, "They're all decked out and ready for bear!" A smashing looking young couple stepped out of their truck.

I waved and yelled, "You guys look like a glossy full page ad for *Outdoor Life* magazine!" They returned grand movie star smiles. A dazzling contrast to our company of rough and scruffy miners and dusty battered trucks and equipment. Soapy wagged her tail and went to greet them. We shook hands and introduced ourselves. My sandpaper rough wrinkled hands and worn down nails, touched the soft scented manicured hands. The boots I wore were held together with duct tape. I'm never embarrassed by my appearance, but perhaps I should be.

The young coastal Californians were tired of smog, traffic, stifling careers, and a mortgage. And were in search of ways to survive outside their careers and city. Paul and Charlene had a $700,000 mortgage; their home at this time they explained only had a $500,000 resale value. And a new truck and camper payment, and credit cards added to their debt load.

None of us desert and river rats had any real debt. No credit cards, no truck payments, no mortgage, no kids in college, actually no kids at all. All of us quite free and unencumbered.

These young Californians were bright, cheerful, quick learners, hard workers, and wanted to try their hands at gold mining. Uncle Wayne had extra shovels, and Texas Jack extra plastic buckets (off limits to myself and the donkeys), so we gladly agreed to a five-way split.

We went to town about once a month. Paul and Charlene (who we referred to lovingly as the Hollywoods) went to town every other day. I'd eat sardines or leftover catfish for breakfast, and pancakes or a peanut butter sandwich with green beans (eaten out of the can) for dinner. The Hollywoods thought our camp menu disgusting—we didn't mention the snake steaks, enjoyed during the summer season or the lion jerky—so they treated us a few times to souffles, luscious soups, breast of chicken in white sauce, radish sprout salads, merlot wine, and frozen peach yogurt.

Though they mentioned difficulty finding most the menu items without driving less than one-hundred fifty miles.

After digging, hauling, and wallowing in mud and muck for almost two weeks, we split out haul of nearly two ounces of gold, five ways. Plus we'd found old marbles, silverware, bottles, and three turquoise nuggets, which held no interest to Paul and Charlene. We could survive on limited recovery of gold and treasure, Paul and Charlene could not. We bade them goodbye and we wished each other luck. The donkeys brayed sadly as they drove away. They'd miss the extra attention, but mostly they'd miss the fresh carrots tops, leftover raisin cinnamon bread, poppyseed muffin oatmeal cookies . . .

## BOILED MULE
### January 2002, Granite Gap

I read a battered issue of *Old West* magazine while sitting in the three sided roofless outhouse, sipping coffee from a tin cup and enjoying the sweepmg view of Granite Gap Mountain. (If I still lived in the Okanogan Highlands I'd be perched on a Styrofoam seat in ten degree weather, with a sweeping view of snow and more snow.) This desert winter morning temperature was probably fifly degrees. Warm by northern standards but not warm by reptile and insect standards. The hand painted outhouse sign I posted a few years ago, *ATTENTION: Watch out for rattlesnakes, coral snakes, Gila monsters, centipedes, ticks,, black widows, tarantulas, horned toads, red ants, fire ants, scorpions, before being seated*; had no impact at the moment.

Winter in the Southwest is a stark contrast to the story in *Old West* titled: *Disaster In The San Juans, Fremont Party 1848*. Blizzards, below zero temperatures, deep snow. Despite this somebody had a sense of humor and wrote in their journal something like this:

BILL OF FARE, CAMP DESOLATON
Dec 25 1848
-MENU-
<u>SOUP</u>

Mule Tail
### FISH
Baked White Mule — Boiled Gray Mule
### MEATS
Mule Steak, Fried Mule, Mule Chops, Broiled Mule, Stewed Mule, Boiled Mule, Scrambled Mule, Shirred Mule, French-fried Mule, Minced Mule
### DAMNED MULE
Mule on Toast (without the toast)
Short Ribs of Mule with Apple Sauce
(without the Apple Sauce)
### RELISHES
Black Mule, Brown Mule, Yellow Mule,
Bay Mule, Roan Mule
### BEVERAGES
Snow, Snow-water, Water.

The consumed mules weren't plump juicy grain fed animals, but gaunt, starving, tough as old boots. I looked at Shaggy, Willy, and me, all plump and well fed. I mentioned to the donkeys standing nearby, "What the hell was John C. Fremont doing with thirty some men and over a hundred mules in the Rocky Mountains blazing trails in winter? A third of the men died and all the mules!" The donkeys looked at me bored, while I babbled on. "We'll wait for summer to prospect in twelve thousand foot elevations!"

Outhouse moments, the only moments Uncle Wayne and Texas Jack allowed me any peace and quiet. The constant activity and debates over trivial matters left me no time to read, watch the birds, brush the donkeys, take long walks or extended coffee breaks. When alone I missed my partners, but when I had constant companions I missed being alone. I could kill Jess, our microbiologist friend for bringing up this micro-fine gold business. Now Uncle Wayne had a new vibrating drywasher with heat blower and crevice suction device combination to work the washes at Granite Gap.

"Damn it you guys," I whined. "We are drywashing at a silver, copper and zinc mine, not a gold mine..."

"But," Uncle Wayne interrupted, "we do have gold here!"

"OK, OK, you're right," I said, "but the stuff's so fine we need Jess's microscope to see it! If I can't see it with my ten power jeweler's loupe, it's too damn small. Mining even a pennyweight will take forever. Besides that I've got a headache and my back is killing me! I don't want to do this."

I paused and scratched Soapy's head, she wagged her tail and seemed interested in our debate. "I vote for going underground hunting specimens of hydrozincite and the other fluorescent minerals those dealers were so excited about." Our rule: not working underground alone was at times stifling.

Uncle Wayne said, "I bought this drywasher guaranteed to find fine gold, specifically for our mine I'd really like to see how it works. If it collects this micro-fine stuff, it will work anywhere."

"Alright, you and Texas Jack win. How about drywashing here for one week. If we can't get at least one ounce of gold with all three of us working then we move our operation to known gold producing areas or go underground to collect. Agreed?"

"Agreed." Uncle Wayne said.

Texas Jack worked nearby adjusting the new drywasher, grinning but silent. His theory, "Always stay out of family disputes." Smart man.

I got my shovel and grumbled to myself, "Maybe I'll go work at McDonalds, or count beans somewhere . . . only work eight hours, five days a week, have running water, hot showers, electric lights . . . go to a chiropractor every week, and get a hair cut at a beauty parlor." I cut my own hair and it looked like it. I sighed and gazed longingly into the distant horizon, the endless valley, the spectacular snow dusted peaks and rhyolite canyons of the Chiricahua's.

Uncle Wayne overheard my musing and laughed heartily, "Forget it Jill. You're unemployable. You'd be bored stiff in two weeks. It'd be like making Calamity Jane work at a boarding school library." Both Uncle Wayne and Texas Jack roared with laughter.

"Ha, ha." I replied and resumed digging down to, and scraping the caliche (our form of false bedrock here in the desert) for microfine paydirt to bounce and vibrate over the new drywasher's riffles. "This is ridiculous," I grumbled to myself, "It will take twenty years to get one ounce of gold . . . damn idiots . . . feel like I'm in the army . . . dig a ditch . . . fill it in . . . you've got nothing better to do . . . I hate you guys."

Then it happened. I broke through a thin layer of caliche, usually hard and thick as a concrete slab, and found a hole, an empty black space. Weird, I thought to myself, Could be a snake den for all I knew. I got a flashlight and peered in.

Looked like large bones and scraps of leather. I started digging around the hole for a better view. By then Texas Jack had come over, curious, then Uncle Wayne. The drywasher was temporarily shut down, and we all started digging. Somehow my headache and backache disappeared. A miracle.

"That's horse bones and a Mexican saddle!" said Texas Jack.

We cleared the dirt away to expose the bones. There were still patches of dried hide and sorrel horse hair. We lifted the bones and saddle out carefullly and underneath all this, deteriorated but intact cowhide saddlebags. The leather was brittle and stiff as cardboard. Texas Jack got a dry paintbrush and meticulously brushed the dirt away. Uncle Wayne used a bottle of his homemade leather restoring solution, made up primarily of glycerine, and a cotton rag to soak the leather saddlebags before opening them up.

I was impatient and wanted to force the flaps open and look inside. But I was told the leather might crack and crumble. While waiting I used my three pronged digging tool, and garden trowel to dig inside the collapsed hole. I found one Mexican silver inlayed etched spur, and smaller bones. The horse skull or any other skull, gone.

Finally we opened the saddlebags and found a few crude Mexican silver coins and scraps of sepia stained paper with faded blue ink hand penned with a quill. Unfortunately the date was hard to read, "1850 or 1860" something. And what looked like a miniature leather suitcase which contained a traveling inkwell and two dipping pen nibs.

We dug and sifted till dark and found a few more treasures. I mentioned selling my share of the loot; so Uncle Wayne and Texas Jack made an offer I couldn't refuse.

Around the campfire, over dinner, we speculated on what happened here long ago. We found no bullets, no parts of a flintlock rifle or cap and ball, no knife, no arrowhead. The horse's leg bones unbroken.

A vivid dream that night under a rustler's moon, of a young dark haired man wearing a new but dusty derby hat, worn pea jacket, gloves and brogans riding a sorrel gelding, clip-clopped past the mine shack. I heard the faint squeak of leather. The sound faded away as rider and horse walked into the freshly excavated hole and disappeared.

The next morning we put all the bones back in the hole and covered them up. It was almost like a funeral. Shaggy and Willy stood nearby watching, silent as ghosts. Soapy, the mine dog sat up straight, alert, unblinking. Uncle Wayne shifted and his shovel clinked on rock, the silence of our mortality was broken. He said, almost in a whisper, "May they rest in peace."

*The Adventures Continue. . .*

## EPILOGUE

Occasionally someone asked, "What happened to that jack you had in Colorado?" or "The kids and I used to stop at Granite Gap with carrot and apple treats to see your two jennies and their spunky foals. Where are they now?"

I'd pour my inquiring guest some coffee, settle back under the ramada and tell him or her about Bosephus the jack, the jennets, Sarah and Lacey, and their jack foals, Dusty and Bandito.

Shaggy and Willy stood nearby and brayed, hoping for handouts while I talked about their old donkey friends.

*The summer in Colorado where I did underground mine tours and ran a gold panning booth* . . . A carload of tourists stopped at the Hard Tack Mine. "Did you lose a donkey? We saw a reddish-white one walking to town dragging a twenty foot rope."

"Oh, no! Not again?" I said. "Thanks for letting me know. I'll go get him."

"Do you want a ride?" the wife in the front seat asked. "Then we can follow you back. Safer that way." She saw the *why would you want to do that* look on my face. "Oh, but we'd love to. It would be exciting for us."

Klondike Mike was on a mine tour. My mom was not in her tent, probably still out collecting wildflower specimens for her botanical studies. I left a note and put up a "BACK IN ONE HOUR" sign. The Hard Tack Mine was fifteen hundred feet above and three miles west of Lake City. Bosephus, our Jack was headed to town, again.

Shaggy, Willy, Sarah and Lacey (the pregnant jennets) were content in their portable polywire two acre corral bordering a creek. I moved this corral to fresh ground every week or so. But Bosephus, the jack, was not content.

Bosephus, a mellow twenty some year old white looking roan donkey, was still an intact breeding jack. *The Definitive Donkey, A Textbook on the Modern Ass* in a chapter subtitle "Handling Uncastrated Jacks" Betsy and Paul Hutchins wrote: " . . . Jacks, unlike stallions are not particularly nervous animals. This makes the handling of a jack a matter for some thought." The authors cite an example. An experienced horseman used to the behavior of stallions was lulled into carelessness by the gentle and truly loving nature of his jack. The man walked into the jack's stall smelling of mares. The jack attacked him by grabbing the handler's arm with his teeth and shook him. Luckily the attack was intercepted.

A provoked jack will grab a gelding, another jack, or human by the teeth shake, then kneel on the victim and proceed to tear him apart. Smell is the main trigger for most animals, much more than sight or sound.

For emphasis the authors wrote, "ALWAYS BE ALERT AND AWARE OF THE NATURAL REACTIONS WHEN HANDLING AN ENTIRE JACK. NEVER LET YEARS OF KINDNESS AND GENTLENESS BLIND YOU TO THE FACT THAT HE IS A MALE EQUINE WITH INSTINCTIVE REACTIONS THAT MIGHT BE DANGEROUS TO A HUMAN OR ANOTHER EQUINE, ESPECIALLY ANOTHER JACK OR A GELDING."

Bosephus hadn't behaved hormonal yet, but had the ability to untie knots and escape hot polywire fences, then he'd walk jauntily three miles to town only to be caught braying and guzzling beer outside the saloon door. This was very entertaining and funny at first, but after three trips up the winding mountain road, 9,000 plus feet above sea level, dragging a resistant jack, I'd had enough. Using the stock trailer to 'haul his ass home' was out of the question, the trailer was now our basecamp storage unit. So when Gene and Mary, business owners in Lake City, offered to buy Bosephus – after seeing their acreage, corrals, barns, cattle and horses – I said yes. They owned a bull and stallion and wanted Bo to breed mares for mules. Perfect. I was not equipped to keep a jack.

Three months later at Granite Gap, Sarah and Lacey each had jack foals a day apart. One brown like mom, the other a gray dun. David, a mineral collector and a regular visitor at the mine, had a place on the Gila River. He fell in love with the jennets and their burritos and offered me $1,800 cash. He had all four vaccinated, the young jacks gelded and bought new western tack for Sarah and Lacey.

Jennets, though as a rule smarter than jacks or geldings, often have dramatic monthly temperament changes which caused problems for me on road and pack trips.

Numerous people offered to buy Shaggy because of his spot coloring, and Willy because of his perfect donkey confirmation and disposition. The geldings Shaggy and Willy and Soapy the mine dog, suited me perfectly and are still with me. We look forward to many more adventures and another book available in 2007.

Laura Leveque<br>
Alias *Jackass Jill*

## APPENDIX A

## ORE DEPOSITS OF
## THE SAN JUAN MOUNTAINS

Most tunnels and drifts were run in on exposed veins. If warranted a shaft was driven, but tunnels were better; full ore carts rolled and water drained from the mines by gravity rather than pumps. No hoists, buckets, and steam engines needed.

The ore deposits in the San Juans are generally grouped as silver bearing fissure veins, gold bearing fissure veins, replacement deposits in quartzite, and replacement deposits in limestone. We saw wide silver bearing fissure veins with well defined foot walls and hanging walls.

The usual minerals in this region are: native gold, gold bearing pyrite, tetrahedrite, chalcopyrite, argentiferous galena, galena with gray copper, ruby silver, brittle silver, and rhodochrosite. We found specimens of all the above except native gold. The most abundant in the area we worked was argentiferous galena (silver and lead galena).

Dr. Edgar B. Heylmun, geologist, states that "placer gold can be found in almost any creek or gulch which drains the Colorado Mineral Belt, and small high-grade placer deposits can still be found, even in districts which have been intensely prospected in the past."

Colorado has produced over 2 million troy ounces of raw placer gold and more than 38 million troy ounces from hard rock extraction. Colorado ranks seventh in production among the West's placer regions, far behind California's top ranked Sierra Nevada gold belt, where placer output alone has topped 60 million ounces.

In Colorado silver was king and millions more ounces of silver were mined from hard rock than gold. We decided hauling hundreds of pounds of silver ore to sell was easier and more cost effective than working all summer for maybe a half ounce of placer gold.

Prospectors searched during the 1850s usually for placer gold. Gold tellurides often left untouched, green gold caused by "impurities" of copper and silver discarded as junk, and silver not easily discovered because the mineral turns green-black, gray, or brown when exposed to the elements. Kind of like leaving your silverware in the hog pen for a few years.

Placer gold was found according to some historians in the 1840s, then further exploration and discovery in the 1850s, and the gold stampede to Pike's Peak in 1859. At this time the Ute Indians owned these mineralized mountains and no legal claims were filed before 1873 when the Utes "sold" the land to the United States. The '59ers gold rush was followed by the 1870s silver boom.

## MINING CAMPS – TOURIST MECCAS

We visited ghost towns, mining camps, and tourist revived towns—none were below 8,250 feet. Animas Forks 11,200 feet, Mineral Point 11,750 feet, Carson on the Continental Divide. Most the ghost towns we saw required crossing four-wheel drive mountain passes 12,000 to 13,000 feet above sea level. Our camp near the ghost town of Henson and the Ute-Ulay Mine 9,200 feet. Mountain villages boast elevation not population. Large quantities of gold, silver, and other precious minerals such as carnotite that have produced millions of dollars in uranium, vanadium, and radium still exist in the mineral belt of Colorado. Most hardrock mines have closed due to the high price of production and foreign market competition (not hamstrung by over-regulation) rather than lack of ore. Now we mine the pockets of tourists from all over the world with a new version of Bill Cody's Wild West Show.

## *APPENDIX B*

## THE HARD TACK MINE HISTORY
### Lake City, Colorado

The Hard Tack Mine tunnel was driven in 1900. The tunnel was to intersect the vein found in the Hidden Treasure Mine one thousand feet higher on the mountain.

The Hidden Treasure mine was established in the 1870s. Landslides and accidents made it difficult to access and unpopular to keep open.

On June 23, 1900 at 3 a.m. an explosion in the Hidden Treasure Mine killed 2 miners. This accident was gruesome. A fellow miner stated, ". . . the head and chest and arms [of the miners] were blown away."

Then on July 2 another miner was killed when the elevator cage jumped the track following another explosion. These were only a few of the fatal accidents which occurred during the Hidden Treasure's history. These closely spaced accidents disrupted the morale of the miners and dropping metal prices ended further tunneling in the Hidden Treasure, as well as the Hard Tack and most mineral belt silver mines.

The California Mine was also a crosscut access tunnel to the Hidden Treasure vein., and is located about one-half mile west of the Hard Tack Mine. The California goes into the depths of the mountain about 900'.

*Sources of information from*
*Delmer Brown and George Hurd, mine owners/operators.*

## *APPENDIX C*

## THE GHOSTS OF ROSEDALE AND ITS MINES

The Rosedale Mining District is in the northern part of the San Mateo Mountains, about 33 miles south west of the Magdalena Mining District. According to the New Mexico Bureau of Mines the first discovery was made in 1882 and production continued until 1916. Although local relatives of pioneers said the Rosedale Mine was worked by the Spanish who "only took out the pillars."

Valentina Lewis, now in her eighties worked at the Rosedale Mine until 1940. Valentina's parents were early homesteaders and ranchers near Rosedale, and later in 1910 opened the Salome General Store in Magdalena. It is still run by Carlotta Salome and her son Nick Sais. Valentina Lewis and Carlotta are sisters.

The Salome General Store is an old time country store. They sell saddles, boots, feed, dry goods, local produce, groceries, and have an old fashioned meat counter. A Magdalena treasure and historical place.

There was no known placer production in Rosedale. Although Nick Sais saw gold nuggets old timers showed him from Rosedale. They could have been amalgamated nuggets or "buttons" because the ore in this area occurs as a manganese-stained quartz in well defined shear zones in rhyolite porphyry. The silicified outcrops stand out clearly. The ore is entirely oxidized, and sulfides are absent. The cyanide leach ponds are white unlike the leach ponds of sulfide ores, which are rusty yellow.

Production figures are sketchy, but the New Mexico Bureau of Mines estimates the Rosedale District produced 27,750 ounces of gold and 10,000 ounces of silver. The miners and owners were rumored to be secretive.

## *APPENDIX D*

### ELIMINATE CINCH SORES FROM YOUR DONKEYS
(AND OTHER BARREL BACKED EQUINES)
Reprinted from
*The Messenger, Catron County News* July 13, 1999

The donkey (and other round back equines) with virtually no withers and possessing a pot belly is prone to the cinch working its way to the very place, against the front legs, where constant movement can rub awful looking sores. I assumed this was one reason donkeys weren't used much for riding.

I tried tight breeching (butt harness), results, cinch galls and raw rumps. My solution for riding and packing was towing another donkey behind the one I was riding. This kept the front cinch pulled back enough to reduce galling. The last animal in the string would require a perfectly balanced pack and a looser than normal cinch which eased friction burns somewhat. This technique worked great on one day five-hour rides, but after three nine-hour days in the saddle, my donkeys were sore.

Most pack and riding saddles made for donkeys and ponies do not address this problem, and are merely smaller size versions of horse tack.

Curley Bowden and Tony Trujillo, both Magdalena New Mexico horse traders, wranglers, mule skinners, wagon masters, solved the donkey cinch dilemma decades ago. They simply buckled the breeching strap that normally attaches to the saddle to the front cinch. (See fig.) They place the saddle back a few inches farther than appears normal, cinch up loosely, snug up breeching, then tighten cinch. Tony likes his britchin' high on the rump, Curley puts his lower at the indentation between the leg and rump.

I prefer this butt strap lower on jennets (so they can pee), higher on geldings.

Now I can pack and ride 8 or 9 hours every day if I want, without waiting a week or two between outings for the donkeys to heal. Thanks Curley and Tony.

(Graphic redrawn from an illustration by Cindy Gonzalez)

## APPENDIX E

## A FEW MINING TERMS

**ADIT** – usually a tunnel run in on an exposed vein, or an entrance to a **DRIFT** - (a dead end tunnel usually following a vein of ore).

**BACK** – is the roof or ceiling of a tunnel. **RIBS** are the sides or wall of a tunnel.

**COLLAR** – the opening of a hole or tunnel in a mine.

**WORKING FACE** or **FACE** – end of the tunnel you are working in.

**CHUTE** – usually a wood structure for holding muck as it falls from a raise or shaft after blasting. Then the chute door is opened and the rock is dumped into the waiting ore car.

**DOUBLE JACK** – a sledge hammer that requires both hands to swing. Usually one miner would hold the drill steel and rotate it after every swing of the double jack.

**SINGLE JACK** – a one handed sledge hammer used to hit the drill steel held in the other hand. This early mining method was used to drill a series of holes in the rock face to place black powder or dynamite. Most frontier tunnels and shafts were driven this way. Modern mines use Pneumatic Rock Drills.

**HANGING WALL** – the wall opposite the foot wall. The ore vein is usually between these two walls and appears to be hanging from the hanging wall.

**HARD HAT** – historically made of cloth or leather and coated with resin.

**MUCK** – any kind of broken rock or valuable ore left after blasting.

**MUCK CAR** – is any type of mine wagon that hauls muck out of the mine.

**A MUCK STICK** – is a shovel of any kind.

**MUCKER** – is a man or machine that shovels ore or waste rock into mine cars for dumping outside the mine or for milling.

**MILLING** – usually entails crushing, heating, and separating valuable minerals from its host rock.

**ORE** – is any rock that bears a saleable mineral.

**PISS DITCH** – is the low side of the tunnel. Most tunnels sloped to one side and downward toward the entrance (away from the face) to get rid of seeping water and full ore cars rolled easily on this slight slope. Some tunnels, usually in arid climates, (ie. Granite Gap) lack seeping water but still slope toward the entrance. The ore cars here were pushed by hand and/or pulled by donkeys.

**RAISE** – a vertical shaft that starts underground and is then mined upwards.

**SKIP BUCKET** – a bucket hooked to a cable so you can hoist supplies and rock up and down a raise or shaft.

**STOPE** – to mine (stope out) the ore between hanging wall and foot wall.

**OPEN STOPE** – is ore mined between the walls vertically up the vein. (This creates a room like cavernous area underground.) The broken ore lands on the rail track and is mucked up.

**VUGH** or **VUGG** – a natural cavity. Most mineral bearing tunnels have natural vugs and caverns, and are often times lined with crystals.

**WINDLASS** – a hand operated hoist using a cable or rope to draw a bucket from a mine, was also used for water wells.

**WHIM** – a hoisting device operated by horse, donkey or slave power. A rope or cable is passed over a pulley and around a drum on a vertical shaft provided with a crossbar

**WINZE** – a shaft or inclined passage from one level to another and for ventilation.

## *APPENDIX F*

## AMERICAN DONKEY & MULE SOCIETY TERMINOLOGY

### *DONKEY TERMS*

**Ass** – The correct term for the animal commonly known as the donkey, burro or jack stock. The term comes from the original Latin term for the animal, Asinus. The scientific name is equus asinus. The term "ass" fell into disrepute through confusion with the indelicate term "arse" meaning the human backside. The difference between asses and horses is a species difference. Like the difference between zebras and horses, closely related, but different species and able to interbreed.

**Jack** – The term used for the male of the ass species. Thus, the often used term jackass, the added ass not necessary.

**Jennet** – The correct term for the female ass; Jenny the informal name.

**Burro** – A word taken directly from Spain and refers to the common working donkey found in Spain and Mexico. The term burro is more common west of the Mississippi, and donkey east of the Mississippi.

**Wild Burro:** These are the feral (originally domestic) asses which run wild in the western part of the US. The American Donkey and Mule Society uses the term burro for these animals. They are registered as "Standard Donkey" and the origin and breeding is given as wild burro.

**Donkey:** A word taken from England. Probably comes from the key words "dun," the common color, and "ky" meaning small. In early England the word ass, taken from the Romans, was the word used. Donkey is a relatively modern term.

**Jack Stock:** The plural term for the American Mammoth Jack and Jennet, and are never referred to as donkeys or burros.

**Gelding Donkey:** The proper term for a gelded (castrated) ass. Informally known as a John.

**Spanish Jack or Spanish Donkey:** These terms acceptable only if the animal has written documented proof of importation of itself or its immediate ancestors from Spain. This includes foreign breeds such as Catalonian, Maltese, and Andalusian. The term Spanish is commonly but improperly used to describe a large standard donkey. Although the ancestry of most donkeys in the US is predominately Spanish.

**Mule Jack:** A jackass used to breed horse mares to obtain mule foals.

**Jennet Jack:** A jackass used to breed donkey jennets to produce donkey foals.

**British Terms:** The English Donkey Breed Society abandoned the terms Jack and Jennet and replaced them with stallion donkey and mare donkey. Although the "hinny" (see mule terms) is called a jennet in Britain, she is a mare hinny or Molly in the US.

## MODERN AMERICAN BREEDS OF ASSES

**Miniature Mediterranean Donkey:** Originally imported mainly from Sicily and Sardinia. To be registered as miniatures the donkeys must be under 36 inches at the withers.

**Standard Donkey:** 36.01 inches to 48 inches at the withers, the most common size range of donkeys. Included in this classification is the Small Standard Donkey: 36.01 inches to 40 inches. (This size often has miniature donkey ancestry.)

**Large Standard Donkey:** 48.01 inches up to 54 inches for females and up to 56 inches for males. This size donkey is often used for breeding saddle mules. The Large Standard also a good working and adult riding donkey.

**Mammoth or American Standard Jack Stock:** The world's largest breed of donkey. Females must be 54 or more inches, males 56 or more inches.

**American Spotted Ass:** A pinto or spotted donkey registered with the American Council of Spotted Asses.

## MULE TERMS

**Mule:** The sterile hybrid produced when a male ass (jack) is crossed with a female horse (mare). The mule will have donkey traits like: long ears, narrower body and smaller hooves. The horse often contributes size and speed. A donkey has the tail of a lion or cow. A mule has a horse tail.

**Hinny:** The sterile hybrid produced when a female ass (jennet) is bred to a male horse (stallion). The genetic inheritance is identical to the mule, although a hinny can look more like a horse with long ears. Hinnies are not as common as mules because donkey jennets do not conceive readily or consistently with horse stallions and any resultant foals mature smaller than mule foals.

**Horse Mule:** Term for the male mule, also commonly called a John mule. The sterile horse mule is always gelded. **Mare Mule:** The proper name for a female mule. The common name is Molly mule.

**Mare Hinny and Horse Hinny:** Use the same terminology as the mule.

**Mule Colt and Mule Filly:** A young male or female mule under the age of three.

## MODERN AMERICAN BREEDS OF MULES

**Cotton, Sugar, Mine, . . . mule –** The old breed terms that are not relevant today. The Modern American Breeds are not differentiated so much by size but by the type of mare the mule was bred from.

**Miniature Mule:** 50 inches or less; bred from miniature horse or pony mares.

**Saddle Mule:** Bred from riding horse mares. Has riding type confirmation.

**Pack/Work Mule:** Bred from mares with some draft blood or of heavy work rather than for saddle type confirmation.

**Draft Mules:** Large mules bred from draft mares. Belgian mules are the most common, valued for their bright sorrel color. Percheron, Clydesdale, Shire and other draft breeds are used.

## COLORS

**Colors:** Mules come in all horse colors. Donkeys' color range are more limited but include: chestnut, bay, roan, gray, white, spotted, leopard appaloosa (no blanket coloring), although the most common is gray dun.

## ABOUT THE AUTHOR

Laura Leveque (Levesque) pronounced Lavek, is a freelance outdoor writer and western artist and lives in Deming, New Mexico. She earned a BA from Washington State University and MA at Central Washington State University. Later worked as a land sales agent in Washington state and New Mexico.

Leveque gold mined in Alaska, Idaho, Washington and New Mexico, and has treasure hunted in most western states. She also worked as an underground mine tour guide and outfitter in Colorado and New Mexico. She has written travel and adventure stories for publications such as *Peninsula Post, RV'n Magazine, Gold and Treasure Hunter* magazine, *Southwest On-line* magazine, *Harness Goat Society News,* Sussex, England, *Women and Guns* magazine, *American Survival Guide,* and more.

Laura says:

My memorable childhood was spent horseback, playing cowboys and Indians on an island off the coast of Washington state. When I was nine years old my family took a road trip to Arizona. I kept a display box of Arizona minerals until I went to college in 1970.

After college, I moved to the Okanogan Highlands near the Canadian border. There I did odd jobs, including work as a forest survey technician, locating lost late 1800s section monuments for USGS topographic maps. The Okanogan National Forest is dotted with abandoned and working mines, hardrock and placer. An interest in mining lead me to placer mine for gold on a suction dredge in Alaska.

At that time my companion animals were dogs. I made dog packs, sleds out of old skis, and crude travois constructed from willow branches. The dogs helped me carry or drag supplies to my remote camps. A logger friend let me use his two BLM burros to pack construction equipment to my cabin; I became hooked on the long eared equines.

I moved back to the island farm for about ten years and raised registered Spot and Landrace hogs, and had a small herd of Angus cows, calves and a bull. I sold the bull and boars after training as a swine and bovine artificial insemination technician. But after being kicked off my foot stool numerous times and left dangling helplessly from the rear ends of eight-foot tall Holsteins, I phased out the cow breeding part of my business.

I tried turning my favorite sows into pack pigs, but their curiosity and "root hog or die" attitude turned that plan into sour slop. I remembered the two BLM burros, sold all the livestock, puchased a cabin near the Olympic Mountains, where it rained, and rained, and rained, and bought pack donkeys.

After several camping trips to the Southwest, I realized I did not want to go back to Washington state. I no longer needed the islands, the year round snow-covered peaks, the towering trees, or the rain. So I packed up the dogs, donkeys, cats and moved to New Mexico.

I learned my love of story and reading from my mom, who edits most my stuff before it's published. Thank God.

## ORDER INFORMATION

**TELEPHONE ORDERS    505-495-5012**
**CREDIT CARDS - MO - CHECKS - ACCEPTED**

Email orders:    granitegapmine@yahoo.com
PayPal

JACKASSJUNCTION.NET

AMAZON.COM

OR

JACKASS JUNCTION PUBLISHING
4815 SILVER CITY HWY NW
DEMING NM 88030

$16.95 + $5.50 PRIORITY SHIPPING
$16.95 + $4.00 FIRST CLASS
$16.95 + $3.00 MEDIA RATE

www.ingramcontent.com/pod-product-compliance
Lightning Source LLC
Chambersburg PA
CBHW021003090426
42738CB00007B/636